100 Years of Faith and Fervor

100 Years of Faith and Fervor

A History of the Greek Orthodox Church Community
Of Greater Salt Lake City, Utah 1905-2005

by Constantine J. Skedros

PUBLISHED BY THE GREEK ORTHODOX CHURCH OF GREATER SALT LAKE

279 South 300 West
Salt Lake City, UT 84101

First Edition

ISBN 0-615-12977-3

*This book is dedicated to the early Greek immigrants to America
and to later generations who had the vision to establish
and perpetuate a Greek Orthodox Church in Salt Lake City
that fosters the faith and culture of their motherland.
It also is dedicated to my parents, James and Angeline Skedros.*

Table of Contents

Acknowledgements

The author and editors gratefully acknowledge the contributions of Patricia Comarell for transcribing all the notes compiled by the author for more than 50 years; Philip F. Notarianni, director, and Kent Powell, historian, of the Utah State Historical Society for their historical perspectives, guidance and support, and also the society's helpful library staff; Louis Cononelos and Kennecott Utah Copper, for contributing historic photos of Bingham Canyon and Copperfield; historian Ann Korologos Bazzarone, Vienna, Virginia, for inspiring the use of oral histories, and Louis Thiros, who assisted with the historic photo retrieval effort from the Hellenic Cultural Association Library. The Greek Oral History Collection, Manuscripts Division, J. Willard Marriott Library, University of Utah, Salt Lake City, Utah, provided personal quotes from Greek immigrants and second generation Greek Americans.

Foreword

As historians examine the Greek immigrant experience, it is not surprising that the Greek Orthodox Church stands as the primary institution to support, foster, sustain, and nurture the thousands of immigrants who came from the mainland and islands of Greece to the mountains and valleys of Utah during the Twentieth Century. The Greek Orthodox Church secured the connection to the Greek homeland and the families who remained behind while providing a base for the pursuit of the freedoms, opportunities, and riches immigrants saw as the American Dream. Today, the church continues to preserve and convey to the descendants of these immigrants, the beliefs, traditions, and culture cherished by their forefathers.

One hundred years after its establishment in Utah, the Greek Orthodox Church is one of the most respected religious and cultural institutions in the state. Its members have contributed significantly to the wealth and well-being of the state while the history, culture, and heritage of the Church and its people have enriched the lives of Utahns and expanded their appreciation for religious and ethnic diversity beyond measure.

This centennial anniversary offers a time not only for celebration and commemoration, but also an opportunity to reflect on the experiences of the Greek immigrants as a people and individuals as they met the peculiar challenges and opportunities in their new home. This book is a fine record of those encounters as it uses church minutes, newspaper accounts, documents, oral history excerpts, and photographs to offer an exceptional glimpse of Greek immigrant and religious life. It is a book to be cherished for the heritage it preserves—a book to be read for the individual experiences and human interaction that are revealed in its pages. The book is an invitation to understand and savor the story of a people, a religion, and a culture, whose heritage has helped shaped who we are as Utahns.

For more than a quarter of a century, the Utah State Historical Society and the Greek Orthodox Cathedral on the

Bingham Canyon Main Street, 1910.

corner of 300 South and 300 West have been neighbors. In 1980, the Historical Society moved into the Denver and Rio Grande Depot just a block and a half west of the magnificent Holy Trinity Greek Orthodox Church consecrated in 1925. But more than physical neighbors, the Greek Orthodox Church and the Utah State Historical Society have been partners in the publishing of articles and books, the development of museum exhibits, and the presentation of programs, tours, and other events undertaken to expand an understanding and appreciation for the Greek immigrants, their descendants, and the heritage that has enriched this state so much.

On the one-hundredth anniversary of the founding of the Greek Orthodox Church in Utah, we extend our most sincere congratulations and express our heartfelt thanks to our neighbors, partners, and friends as you begin the second hundred years.

May they be as rich and stimulating as the first hundred years have been.

Allan Kent Powell
Historian
Utah State Historical Society

Preface

In 1945, Salt Lake City native Constantine "Con" Skedros returned home from military service in World War II and began collecting and compiling the rich, often contentious, history of the Greek Orthodox Church and Greek community in Utah. He did it obituary-by-obituary, news clipping-by-news clipping, Parish Council minutes-by-Parish Council minutes. In many instances he was more than chronicler of the events, he was an active participant in their development.

This book is not presented as a comprehensive historical account of the evolution of the church and community—primarily in the Salt Lake area—since record keeping has not always been thorough or even attempted by community leaders. Instead, for the most part, this book is a synopsis of Skedros' work. His is a chronological account of the community's existence in Utah, presented primarily in a series of snippets and enhanced by listings, photos, and graphics. Also enhancing the church accounts are excerpts from quotations taken from oral histories on file at the Special Collection Department of the J. Willard Marriott Library at the University of Utah. The entire compilation—some 400 pages—

of Skedros' massive research undertaking is on file in the main office of the Greek Orthodox Church of Greater Salt Lake and the Hellenic Cultural Museum Library in Salt Lake City.

Since most of the material herein is based upon the author's review of church records, some segments of the evolution of the Greek community have received less attention than they deserve. The selectivity due to that fact is exacerbated by space and production limitations of the book.

The primary editors of this book are members of the parish who are professional journalists experienced in publishing historical materials. They exercised "best judgment" practices in selecting which items among the voluminous material available to include, which to condense, and which to omit. Historical significance, relevance, interest, and an item's propensity to provide a glimpse into the time and tenor of the community were primary factors in the decision-making process.

Editor: Mike C. Korologos
Salt Lake City

Associate Editor: Mary P. Chachas
Salt Lake City

Chris and Marina Dokos and their children, George, left and James, Midvale, Utah, 1910.

100 Years of Historical Highlights

The early years (1900–1955) were very difficult for the Greek immigrants and their families due to hostility, prejudices, discrimination, the Great Depression, and world and regional wars. Perseverance, hard work, and their faith led to their acceptance into the community and—in several cases—to prosperity.

1900	Greek immigrants began to arrive in Salt Lake and Ogden areas
1905	Greek community of Utah organized
	First Holy Trinity Church constructed
1910	"Greek Town" established in downtown Salt Lake City and became center of Greek community.
1915	First Greek school established
1923–25	Current Holy Trinity Church constructed
1925	First Greek Sunday Schools organized
1932–40	Immigrants survived Great Depression
1935	Greek Mothers' Club and Holy Trinity choir organized
1940–45	The War Years
1944	Community purchased property north of Holy Trinity Church to construct cultural center
1948	Modern Greek class offered at University of Utah
1950	Hellenic Memorial Building constructed
1955	50th Anniversary celebration observed

1950s	Greek school built in West Jordan
1958	14th Clergy-Laity Conference held in Salt Lake City
1958–62	Community purchased property north of Holy Trinity Church and two parish homes (later sold)
1962	Community purchased property in southeast area of Salt Lake City (later sold)
1966	Community purchased property at 5335 South Highland Dr.
1968	Construction of Prophet Elias Church began
1969	Prophet Elias Church completed—services began in December
	National Greek Orthodox Youth of America (GOYA) Conference held in Salt Lake City
1972	La France Apartment complex purchased by Greek community
1974	Fund-raising campaign launched to pay off mortgage on Prophet Elias Church
1975	First Greek Festival
	Holy Trinity Church placed in National and State Historical Registers

1977	Crane property on 300 West and 200 South purchased
1980	Underground water seepage problem at Prophet Elias Church eliminated
1977–80	Hellenic Memorial Building expanded
1978–88	All properties north of the Memorial Building owned by Greek community
1977–80	Mosaics added at Prophet Elias Church and improvements made at Holy Trinity Church
1981	Mosaics fell at Prophet Elias Church
1986	Holy Trinity elevated to cathedral status
	Hellenic Cultural Association organized
1987	Diocese of Denver and San Francisco Choir Conference held in Salt Lake City
1988–91	Mosaics at Prophet Elias replaced and iconography replaced
1988	Hellenic Monument dedicated at Holy Trinity Cathedral
1991	Consecration of Prophet Elias Church

1992	Hellenic Cultural Association Museum opened in lower level of Cathedral
	Church garden area at Holy Trinity completed
1993	Festival storage areas added to Hellenic Memorial Cultural Center
1994-97	Multi-purpose center built at Prophet Elias Church
1995	National Young Adult Conference held
1997	St. Sophia Hellenic Orthodox School opened
2000	Hellenic Heritage Campaign began
2002	Community welcomed Olympic Winter Games of 2002
2004	Restoration of Holy Trinity Cathedral began
2005	100th Anniversary of the establishment of Greek community in Salt Lake City observed

Introduction

This book is a history of the first Greek immigrants who came to Utah in 1900, of the formation of the Greek community of Utah in Salt Lake City in 1905, and of the dedication, generosity, frustrations, and festivities that shaped the community that now thrives.

In the fall of 2005, this community, held together by religious beliefs and energized by a zest for life, observed its centennial and honored the faith and fervor that were so prevalent in the early immigrants—and continue to this day. Greeks of this community have weathered—and continue to weather—the financial strains of growth, but also find joy in the accomplishments of the past as they strive, quite successfully, to perpetuate the customs and traditions, religious rituals, and beliefs that have been entrusted to us by our forefathers.

I have been collecting historical materials related to the Greeks' first 100 years in Utah since 1950. My goal has been to present a fair and honest review of events, based primarily upon the workings of the Greek Orthodox Church, which has served as the catalyst for virtually all activities involving the community. My work is far from complete. It is my wish that someone, with the necessary skills in historical research, will build upon what I have compiled and write a more definitive history of our community—one that highlights the cultural, family, and community spirit of the Greeks.

A major obstacle in preparing this book was the lack of significant documents—the early Greeks did not preserve them. In more recent years, members of our community have made notable efforts to collect and preserve such records.

I dedicate this book to those early Greek immigrant men and women, the pioneers, who had the vision and determination to create our community.

One cannot write enough about that first generation of Utah Greeks. Despite discrimination, open hostility and prejudice, they committed themselves to establishing our church-community in the shadows of the Wasatch Mountains, within a city carved out from the wilderness only 58 years

Stained glass windows enhance Holy Trinity Cathedral.

earlier. It was their dream that the mother country's customs, culture, language, and traditions be perpetuated through the Greek Orthodox Church. Their hope was to pass on to future generations that which they created here.

They overcame many obstacles, maintaining a devotion to their native land while becoming loyal and proud citizens of their adopted country—America. That's why I call them our "Greatest Generation of Greeks."

History teaches us about our past, no doubt, but it also helps us to think creatively about ourselves and about our future. It is for all of us to wisely follow in the footsteps of our predecessors who, through personal and family sacrifice, forged our Greek Orthodox community of Salt Lake City.

We have a proud, rich, and majestic cultural and religious heritage. All of us, young and old, and the generations to come, are the architects of today and of the future. How will our accomplishments be judged?

On this, the 100th anniversary of the establishment of the first Greek Orthodox Church in Utah, a viable, dynamic Greek-American community celebrates and, rightly so, as that is the way of the Greeks. The task of keeping the flame alive is passed to the next generation that will face many challenges of its own. But we, as mentors and monitors, are confident that the future "keepers of the flame" will meet their responsibilities with the same faith and fervor as their predecessors.

Today, Greek Orthodoxy and Hellenism in the United States are at a crossroad. Some voices speak out that we should remain as part of the Greek Diaspora and with the Ecumenical Patriarchate. Other voices speak out that the time is approaching for the creation of the American Orthodox Church. Which voice will prevail is unknown. One thing is certain: the Greek Orthodox Church in the United States is changing and will continue to change.

With that change come challenges. Some of the issues I believe our church-community and the Greek Orthodox Church in the United States must address are as follows:

- The unity of the present church-community must be preserved.
- The demographics of the church-community are changing. Immigration from Greece is negligible. The second generation soon will be gone and the second wave of immigrants who arrived here after 1950 will be gone within 20 years. Today, the third, fourth, and fifth generations and converts through inter-faith marriages are in the majority. In 2020, we will be a completely different church-community.
- Membership in the church-community does not mean that one must be Greek. Orthodox Christians represent several ethnic groups, including Russian, Romanian, and Serbian.
- We must continue to make an effort to preserve our Greek Orthodox and our Hellenic heritage. Even though in the future we will be "less Greek," we must preserve our culture, language, and religion. This will not be an easy task.

- We must develop more educational and cultural programs. We excel in dance groups, athletic events, in staging Greek Festivals and the like, but it will take more than such events to save Hellenism and Orthodoxy in our community.

- We need a new and larger cultural center. The church's primary properties are located at 300 South and 300 West, a prime area for growth in Salt Lake City's downtown area. We must enhance our image and presence as a significant religious community in the heart of Salt Lake City.

- We must continue to nurture the activities of the Hellenic Cultural Museum/Library.

- We must continue to nurture the great work being performed at St. Sophia Hellenic Orthodox School.

- We should purchase property in the southwest area of Salt Lake City for a third church that eventually will be needed.

Constantine J. Skedros
Historian, Greek Orthodox Church of Greater Salt Lake 2005

Holy Trinity Cathedral, 279 South 300 West, Salt Lake City, Utah.

The lack of Greek women in Salt Lake City in the early Twentieth Century is evident in this photograph of the Fotis-Zampos wedding on October 19, 1909, taken in front of the original Holy Trinity Church, 439 West 400 South.

Chapter 1

Historical Overview

Among the pioneers of the New World who forged brilliant chapters in the growth and development of America were the European immigrants who came to America after 1800. They came from various parts of the world, but particularly from Europe. They were pioneers in the same sense as the storied and hardy fur-trappers, the gold-seekers, the Indian scouts, the frontiersmen, the cowboys, the homesteaders, and the settlers of this country's Western movement. All of them blazed trails into uncharted territory.

Petro Mastoris and Rosie Karafotias were married in 1918.

European migration to the United States started as a trickle about the 1850s and it became a tidal wave by the early 1920s. The immigrants from southern Europe were some of the last of that era to come to this country. The Greeks were the smallest ethnic group, and one of the last to come to America.

One reason for this belated migration was the fact that for more than 400 years the land of Hellas was under the control of the Ottoman Empire. Until 1453, when the historic city of Constantinople fell to the Ottomans, the Byzantine Empire was the center of Eastern Christianity and civilization, the nurturing ground of the Hellenic culture and language.By 1821, the movement for Greek independence had begun. The goal was achieved in 1829. In the years immediately following that liberation, the Greeks were absorbed in solving problems created by the revolution and in rebuilding a proud nation. Most were preoccupied trying to survive at home—they were not interested in leaving their country for distant shores.

That mindset did not change until the last two decades of the Nineteenth Century. Once migration to America started, however, it did not abate until the early 1920s when federal legislation restricted immigration, especially from southern Europe. In the 1960s, immigration laws were changed, allowing a greater number of Greeks to migrate to America.

Michael Katsanevas, standing, presided over his Greek Coffee House, Anekti Karthia (Open Heart), in Salt Lake City in the 1920s.

These Greeks left their homeland to find work in far-off lands so that they could send money to parents, brothers, and sisters. They hoped their money would help rebuild the village church, hospital, and schools, or prepare a sister's dowry.

Greek immigrants landed first in America's east and southeast sectors. Greek sea captains and cotton merchants in New Orleans organized the first Greek Orthodox Church founded in the United States in 1864. By 1900, New York City, Chicago, Boston, Baltimore, and the textile center of Lowell, Massachusetts, boasted sizable Greek colonies.

For Greeks, life in these cities was centered on a particular section where one could find the old-world transplanted, complete with customs, language, and traditions surviving, even thriving, in the hustle of the New World. The newly arrived immigrants were attracted to closely knit communities where they found people from their home villages, their native language spoken, and the familiar *kafenio*—or coffee house—an important part of Greek social life for men.

It was in these communal centers that the immigrants—men during the first five years—heard about the need for unskilled laborers in places named Bingham Canyon and Castle Gate, Utah; Butte, Montana; Pueblo, Colorado; Pocatello, Idaho; and McGill and Ely, Nevada. They heard of large numbers of their countrymen being employed by the railroad companies to lay tracks in the western part of the

Dire economic prospects and political turmoil in Greece were significant forces that tipped the scales in favor of migrating to the United States. The movement was accelerated by the deep-rooted desire of Greek people to better themselves and to assist loved ones left behind in Greece—in the mountain villages of Epirus and Roumeli, in the fishing villages of the islands in the Aegean and Ionean Seas, in the Peloponnesus, and on the beautiful island of Crete.

country. Within a few years, Greek immigrants had settled in every section of the United States.

The typical early Greek immigrant considered his stay in America to be temporary. He wanted to work in America for a number of years, save his money, and return to his homeland where he would live relatively well. However, the longer immigrants remained in America the more they became accustomed to the ways of American life.

Eventually they became such advocates of the American lifestyle that, with the advent of World War I, they served in

Six Greek-American soldiers in World War I uniform, 1918. Those identified are Charles Dimas, standing left, John Praggastis, and kneeling, James Skedros, center.

the military for their adopted land. By the end of the war, the partial integration of the Greek immigrant was underway. Many of them returned to their native land but the majority decided to make the United States their permanent home.

Archibald McClure, in his book on foreign immigrants, *Leadership of the New America*, said, about the new American citizens of Greek background:

> *…that they are democratic and liberty loving is a trait that should make them valuable citizens, while their regard for education and the fact that most of their leaders are educated men is an important and excellent feature of their American life.*

After World War I, immigrants became more assimilated into American society. Many had married by this time, and the first generation of Americans of Greek descent was enrolled in American schools. Greek businessmen were successfully operating various enterprises, and the immigrants were building churches wherever they settled.

By the time of World War II, Greek immigrants had become proud American citizens. For this war, however, citizen immigrants were too old to volunteer their services; in their places came thousands of young Americans of Greek descent who answered the call of their parents' adopted country to serve in its armed forces.

By the end of World War II, Greek immigrants and their families had totally integrated into American society.

Utah's Early Immigrants Who were the first Greek immigrants to come to Utah? This is a question that cannot be easily answered. No official records are available from which the name or names of the earliest pioneer immigrants can be obtained. However, a United States Census Bureau report lists the number of Greeks in Utah:

1870 — 1 Greek	*1890 — 3 Greeks*
1880 — 2 Greeks	*1900 — 3 Greeks*

Gregory and Maria Halles with their daughter Athena, front center, were hosts at a Christmas dinner in the 1920s. Attendees included Alex Halles, standing left, John Halles; William Pappas, standing, second from right, Katherine Pappas, Stamatina P. Pappas. Seated are George Koukourakis, second from left, Irene Mavrakis holding Georgia, and Alex Halles, second from right.

Mt. Olivet Cemetery burial records of the early Twentieth Century substantiate these names and dates:

November 10, 1901	*Michael Kolsirilos*
July 1, 1903	*John Vacopoulos*
October 5, 1903	*George N. Fillis*
February 10, 1904	*G.N. Antoniou*
August 14, 1904	*Bill Farros*
November 25, 1904	*Charles Makis*
June 5, 1905	*John D. Droulas*

The first Greek to reside in Utah Territory was likely Nicholas Kastro, who was traced to being here in 1870, arriving at the mining camp of Bingham Canyon from California. It appears that he spoke Greek poorly, indicating that he had left his homeland at an early age. His apparent lack of formal education did not prevent him from being a successful miner and prospector. He organized his mining claims, known as the Kastro Group, into the Kastro Grecian Mining Company, and, in 1911, sold the company to a group of his Salt Lake countrymen for a reported $35,000.

There were reports that Kastro also was an Indian fighter and a personal friend of Brigham Young, then the leader of the Church of Jesus Christ of Latter-day Saints (Mormon) whose pioneers settled in the Salt Lake Valley in July, 1847. Kastro's trail disappeared from the Utah scene in 1912, and it was rumored that he returned to his native Greece at the age of 80. Leonidas Skliris, who ultimately gained notoriety as a

Main Street Salt Lake City, 1905.

labor-procurement agent, was likely the second Greek immigrant in the region, arriving in 1898.

The rate of immigrant arrival gradually increased, and by 1902 several hundred Greeks were making their homes in Salt Lake City and Ogden. There were 162 Greek names in the Salt Lake City Directory for 1901–1903, the vast majority listing American Smelting and Refining as their place of employment. By 1904, more than 1,000 Greeks lived in the greater Salt Lake City area, many employed at the various railroad companies laying new tracks and replacing wooden bridges with concrete structures. Others worked at the refineries, mills, and smelters in Midvale, Murray, and Garfield, where small Greek communities blossomed.

Upon arriving in Salt Lake City, Greek immigrants would look for fellow countrymen who might be able to help them find places to sleep, provide them with food, and help them find a job. By 1904, the Greek arrivals settled in an area roughly along First, Second, and Third South Streets between Second and Sixth West Streets, an area that came to be known as "Greek Town," that included newly established Greek businesses. It didn't take long for Salt Lake City's "Greek Town" to become a thriving locale abuzz with commerce.

James Skedros stands at the counter of the Rizos-Skedros Drug Store, 480 West 200 South in the 1920s.

"It was pretty hard to find a Greek lady. Because there were too many boys and less Greek girls. And then, the men who had businesses or had money, that's who was the first choice."

—George Adondakis, b. 1902
Greek Oral History Collection

Business Ventures The first recorded Greek business of any significance in the valley was a wholesale grocery store operated in "Greek Town" by Pete Nikolopoulos, who sold to Greeks throughout the Intermountain Area.

Four Greek businesses were located in downtown Salt Lake in 1903:

1. *The Oriental Candy Company and Kitchen at South Main Street;*
2. *A grocery store at 279 East 300 South, owned by John the Greek (no last name).*
3. *The Athenian Bachelor's Club at 147 South Main Street. This was a kafenio (coffee house), believed to be the first in Salt Lake City; and*
4. *A lunch wagon on Main Street, operated by Vassilios Demos.*

Many bachelors were included in the Salt Lake City Greek population in the early years. Most of them lived in small downtown hotels or rooming houses. Because they were very mobile, moving around for better work, many did not have permanent addresses. This was the period when a growing list of businesses also served as "post offices" for the immigrants. Several members of today's Greek community have recollection of these businesses and their proprietors.

Businesses Serving as Post Offices
for Greek Immigrants

New York Shoe Shine Parlor, 18 West 200 South—
Andy Bathemess

Arcade Barber Shop, 69 West 200 South; also in Greek
Town—Alex Zaharias

Stadium Café, 67 West 200 South—Stelios Kotsolios
(This was the main gathering place for many bachelors.)

Open Heart Kafenio, 540 West 200 South—
Michael Katsanevas; later Louis Perran
(The kafenio later became a café.)

Grecian Bakery, 550 West 200 South—Andrew Dokos

Rizos-Skedros Drug Store, 480 West 200 South—Alex Rizos,
James Skedros

Parisian Bakery, 74 West 200 South—Bill Nicholson

Restaurant-Kafenio, 520 West 200 South—Peter Fotis
(This was one of the first "post offices.")

In 1905, the Greek community in Salt Lake City was all
male. By 1907, with an established church and an ever-
growing "Greek Enclave" in the city, the community was
rapidly changing. Arriving from Greece were the wives,
children, sisters, and brothers of many of the immigrants.
Eventually, the sisters who were single became the prospective
brides for many of the young single men. As a result, family life
was underway with children (the first generation of native-
born Greek Americans) being born in the Salt Lake Valley.

"I had my first papers (citizenship) when I entered the
army. Before we went to the battlefield, they told us to report
to the general headquarters for our papers. They questioned
us and said we can't give your final papers here, but if you
survive the war (1917) you can get your final papers in your
home town and state."

—Theodore Marganis, b. 1892
Greek Oral History Collection

Alex Zaharias, fifth from left, owned this barber shop in "Greek Town" in 1908. John Panagopoulos, fourth from left, is among the barber's associates/friends shown here.

Copperfield Mercantile in the early 1900s.

Wedding, baptismal, and funeral records from 1905 to 1914 mark the increase in size of the community and the development of family life: 100 weddings, 128 baptisms, and 415 funerals were recorded. From 1915 to 1920, there were 469 baptisms recorded. The disproportionate number of funerals, mostly for young males, would indicate a large number of industrial accidental deaths. The figures are for sacraments performed for Greek and other Eastern Orthodox immigrants.

In its centennial year, 2005, the Greek Orthodox Church of Greater Salt Lake had approximately 1,000 dues-paying "steward" families out of an estimated 4,000 Greek Orthodox people in Salt Lake Valley. Price, in Carbon County, numbers some 100 Greek Orthodox families and in Ogden it is estimated that there are 150 active Greek Orthodox families.

"So when I landed in Salt Lake, I went over to the Wilson Hotel...and I got a job there in the kitchen—as a pantryman. Ah, glassware and the silver...I was watching the men who was talking, making the salads and all of the dressings and salads...and all that kind of stuff and I learned how to make all that stuff...

"By the way...at that time we lived down at Phibb's Court, three of us together—three boys in a rooming house. We had a room with three beds and we paid four dollars a month each at Phibb's Court. That's between West Temple and First West and Second South. And work at the Wilson Hotel...have to report at six o'clock in the morning and work till two, and then get off from two to five and come back five and work till eight, nine o'clock every day. That was everyday, full week and every month. And no days off...And the big wages we got. A dollar a day. Thirty dollars a month."

—Harry Miles, b. 1893
Greek Oral History Collection

Communities Established

By 1910, Greeks had established communities in the smelter and mining communities of Murray, Midvale, Copperfield, Garfield, Magna, and Tooele. They had settled in the mining districts of Carbon and Emery counties, in Price, Helper, Hiawatha, Sunnyside, Commerce, and Scofield. A "Greek Town" also was established in Ogden, near the Union Station on 24th and 25th Streets.

By this time, Salt Lake City boasted several first-class restaurants and candy stores operated by Greeks, which thrived until the late 1940s. Gradually, the closely knit ethnic community began to disappear as many of these businessmen sold their establishments, some to return to Greece to live, while others—the greater majority—moved to more favorable business locations in the central business district. By 1960, the capital city's "Greek Town," ceased to exist. The total integration of the Greek businessmen into the American community was complete.

A book written in 1912 by Thomas Burgess, *Greeks in America*, highlights almost all aspects of Greek immigration to the United States, including a description of the Salt Lake City Greek community:

> *About 5,000 people are in the State of Utah, most of them workmen in the coal and other mines and on the railway lines. The chief center is Salt Lake City. At present there are some one hundred Greek businesses; and consist of coffee houses, restaurants, groceries, saloons, barber shops. The rest are candy stores, and boot black stands.*

Enterprising Businessmen The early Greeks were enterprising. Where there was work, they took it. They also created their own employment. Between 1905 and 1960 hundreds of Greek immigrants owned small enterprises. They included grocery stores, confectioneries, drugstores, and a variety of eating places. Shoe shine parlors, cleaners and tailors, hat shops, bars, rooming houses/apartments/hotels, theaters, lumber and coal yards, livestock businesses, and manufacturing were also thriving enterprises.

The family of George and Angeline Chipian Kanell is an example of such entrepreneurship. George Kanell opened his first grocery store in Bingham Canyon in 1918. When he moved to Salt Lake City, he opened a store on the corner of 200 West and 700 South. He died in 1931, but his widow operated the store until her death in 1974, and their children then operated it until the 1980s. In addition, family members have operated J-Burger, Kanell TV, and Kanell Furniture and Appliance.

Brothers Gus and Charles Paulos, in Magna, started an automobile dealership in 1921. Upon Gus' death, sons Ernest and Peter assumed the business. The founder's grandson, and namesake, operates today's Gus E. Paulos Auto Dealership.

In the 1920s and 1930s, brothers George N. and Louis N. Strike, and business partners George Zeese and John Gerendas, were notably successful. George N. Strike, older brother of Louis, owned the Murray Laundry, one of the

The original and popular Politz Candy Company occupied the northwest corner at 300 South and State Street in the 1920s. Among those shown are Ernest Mantes, far left, George Karras, Mrs. Tom Politz, fourth from left, Tom Politz, and Pete Bazoukis, far right.

"In our family, we had a little red chair in the store. And one of us would sit on the little red chair—the smallest of us would sit on the red chair and hand up the candy to my dad when he'd sell it over the counter… that's where we all started, on that little red chair."

—John Chipian, b. 1923
Greek Oral History Collection

Louis N. Strike founder of the Western Laundry Press and Ajax Press.

largest in Salt Lake County, and the Strike Fruit Farm in Holladay. He became an owner and operator of laundries in Southern California during World War II.

In 1929, Louis N. Strike founded the Western Laundry Press, which manufactured laundry equipment sold worldwide under the name of Ajax Press. The Strike sons, Nicholas L., John L., and George L., joined the business after World War II. Peak employee total at the plant in the late 1960s was 600, many of them Greeks. The Ajax plant closed in 1975 and its operations moved to Cincinnati, Ohio, where George L. Strike became president of the American Laundry Machinery Co. and minority owner of the Cincinnati Reds, major league baseball team.

George Zeese and John Gerendas, who were in the grocery store business in Carbon County, Utah, moved to Salt Lake City in 1933, and by the end of 1934 had opened five large Success Markets. During the next 10 years, they operated eleven supermarkets. In the late 1940s, Gerendas started his own chain, the Crystal Palace. Zeese continued to expand his enterprise until the 1950s when he sold his interest in Success Markets to the Albertsons and Smith's chains.

Prominent Greek Entrepreneurs from 1905–1950 included: Tom Politz,
confectioneries; Alex Rizos, James Skedros, drug stores; George Tahtaras, restaurants; George Lamb and Ted J. Speros,

Lamb's Grill Café; Peter E. Athas, drug store; Chris Athas, drug store; John Condas, sheep and land; John A. Ypsilantis, sheep; Jim Kumarelas, Magna mercantile, land; Emanuel, William, and George Papanikolas, lumber and coal yards, later auto dealership; Ernest Mantes family, auto dealerships, Tooele; Nick Lendaris, George Adondakis, Nick Kouris, mercantile in Bingham Canyon; Tom Praggastis, Charles Dimas, Ernest Chipian, and Chris Apostol, Bingham Canyon grocers; Chris Bapis, Christ Pappasotiriou, George Pappasideris, Copperfield grocers; James Daskalakis, bakery; Milton and Harry Stamoulis, auto dealerships in Magna and Price; James Latsis, Sportsman's Supply Company, Black Rock Beach, real estate; Souvall brothers (William, Jim, Pete), coal yards, restaurants, bars, wholesale distributing; John Zekas, sheep, bars in Price and Salt Lake; George Floor, Andy Floor, Dan Kostopulos, John Kerikas, and Michael Siouris, movie theater owners/operators.

Greek-owned Businesses in Salt Lake City, 1904–1950*

YEAR	GREEK TOWN	CENTRAL BUSINESS DISTRICT	TOTAL
1904	20	12	32
1908	37	27	64
1912	87	46	133
1916	116	78	194
1922	112	134	246
1931	50	110	160

—*Utah Gazetteer*

*By 1950, 275 Greek businesses operated in the Greater Salt Lake Valley, as researched by Constantine J. Skedros. (See Resource List, page 147.)

Business Expansion Beyond Utah

Greek immigrants and their descendants continued to make their mark in business enterprises from 1950 onward. Nicholas and Company, a nationally acclaimed food distribution company that still operates in the Intermountain West, was founded in 1940 by Nicholas Mouskondis, whose son Bill is chief executive officer.

The sons of Emanuel Papanikolas—John, Nick, Gus, and Spiro—were principals in Cannon-Papanikolas Construction Company, a major builder of homes and shopping centers in the Salt Lake Valley. After buying the Conquistador Hotel complex in Tucson, Arizona, they developed a major golf course and shopping center there. The Titan Steel Company in Salt Lake City and lumberyards in Baker, Oregon, were among their interests.

Ted, John, Mike, and Steve Sargetakis founded Silver State Suppliers, a wholesale distributor of fabrics with business throughout the United States, in Salt Lake City in 1952. Steve's wife Kaliope, and his sons, Manoli, Ted, and John operate the business.

Souvall Brothers Wholesale Distributors, organized by brothers Andy, Sam W., George and Peter W. Souvall, and John Billinis did business throughout the Intermountain West. After selling this company, they branched out in such businesses as record distributing, banking, commercial real estate, and construction.

Bingham Canyon native Nick S. Vidalakis and his family built and managed large shopping centers named Family Centers in Salt Lake City, and Davis counties in Utah, and in Idaho and Nevada.

Christ Pappasotiriou (Sotiriou) moved his family to Salt Lake City after operating a grocery in Copperfield, Utah. The Broadway Shopping Center was opened in 1952 and was the first in the Salt Lake Valley to have a pharmacy within the grocery store. Sons Gus and Tommie, both pharmacists, and siblings Margo and Leo, were active members of the business

The Palace Candy Company, at 245 South Main Street, boasted an elegant interior. Owner was James A. Moore (Maroudas).

Lamb's Grill Cafe, Salt Lake City, 1940s.

which expanded to include providing pharmaceuticals to nursing homes, and real estate investments.

Lamb's Grill, a landmark on Salt Lake City's Main Street, is owned and operated by John Speros, son of Ted J., early and long-time owner. Gregory Skedros, a pharmacist who turned his cooking talent to the restaurant business, founded the Mandarin restaurant in Bountiful in 1978. Jim Fuskundrakis operates eight Jim's Family Restaurants, and the Tony

"…there was a big strike at Utah copper…and eventually most of these people had to leave…and my dad who had the slaughter house was stuck with some 500 lambs and they became a year old and they're called yearlings and you can't sell them as lamb. …So fortunately he got some rams and got in the sheep business."

—George Condas, b. 1914
Greek Oral History Collection

Kefalopoulos family owns Olympic Grills in the Salt Lake valley. Other families also in the restaurant enterprise are Nick Liotiris, Anthony Kartsonis, Nick Papadakis, Angelo Brillos, Demetri Politis, John Marinos, Deno Priskos, John Nikols, George Chichis, Sam Bournakis and Jim Tsoufakis.

During the 1960s–1980s, a new wave of Greek immigrants to Utah made a lasting impression. The fast food business is significantly represented by some of these Greeks: John and Michael Katzourakis and Manuel Katsanevas family, Crown Burger; Effichios Katsanevakis and John Hatzipolakis, Atlantic Burger; John Lyhnakis family, Astro Burger; Neofitos family, Olympic Burger; Lee Paulos and Pete Koukoulias families, Greek Souvlaki; Jerry Ziakas family, The Mad Greek; John Ziouras family, The Bakery, Apollo Burger; Angelo Tsoutsounakis family, Astro Burger; Kostas Luras, The Other Place; Yanni Armaou, Yanni's Greek Express; Mike Limanzakis, The Greek Market; Jim and Mike Mylonakis, International Pantry.

John Saltas is president/executive editor of Copperfield Publishing Inc., which publishes *Salt Lake City Weekly*, an alternative newspaper available free at 1,800 locations.

The strong work ethic of the early Greeks and their commitment to bettering themselves through education and ingenuity was passed on to their descendants. Subsequent generations of Greek Americans are well represented in the business arena and are found in medicine, law, dentistry, engineering, education, finance, and other professions.

Ethnic miners, mainly Greeks, gather at the portal of an underground mine in Bingham Canyon, Utah, 1904–1906.

Labor Front In 1903, an event of major importance to the growth and development of the State of Utah occurred. It was the opening of a copper mine at Bingham Canyon, 17 miles southwest of Salt Lake City in the Oquirrh Mountains. Known as Utah Copper and then as Kennecott Copper, to reflect its owner at the time, this massive mining operation had a tremendous effect on the lives of foreign-born immigrants, especially the Greeks.

With the opening of the mine came a call for unskilled laborers, those accustomed to backbreaking work. Thousands of immigrants flocked to the copper operation in Bingham Canyon and to the smelters of Salt Lake County and Tooele to do the work that eventually led to the formation of an industrial empire. Included in this large labor force, and constituting perhaps the largest single ethnic group, were the Greeks.

At the same time, the coal and coke mines of Carbon and Emery Counties, and nearby areas, issued calls for unlimited numbers of laborers because of a strike by Italians, Slavs, and Finns. As in the case of the copper mines, immigrants, especially Greeks, migrated to the coalfields to perform the spadework that led to a thriving mineral extraction industry in Utah.

By 1910, Greek immigrant labor had become a significant force in the greater Salt Lake area as well as in the Intermountain West.

A central figure in this phenomenon was Leonidas Skliris, a labor-procurement agent for several of the major enterprises in the area, including Utah Copper Company, the Denver & Rio Grande Railroad, the Western Pacific Railroad, and coal mines in Carbon and Emery Counties. Through his associates in the mining, railroad, and smelter towns, he collected a dollar-a-month fee from each immigrant for whom he found a job. Almost all the laborers paid this fee for fear of losing their jobs, and Greek immigrants who were "encouraged" to buy their groceries and other goods from his enterprises supplemented Skliris' income. These practices continued for several years, eventually leading some of the laborers to speak out against the unscrupulous activities of Skliris, the so-called "Czar of Greek labor."

Leonidas Skliris,
"Czar of Greek labor," 1913.

Mines, Railroads Draw Greeks, 1905–1920

The contributions of hard-working Greek immigrants can be measured by the following estimated figures of Greeks employed in mining and railroads between 1905 and 1920:

1910: nearly 1,000 Greeks at Magna-Garfield smelters;
400 at Midvale smelter;
400 at Murray smelter;
1912: 1,210 Greeks at Utah Copper Company, constituting approximately 35 percent of its labor force. During World War I, this number grew to 1,500;
1915: 200–300 Greeks at Tooele smelter;
1916–1918: 1,500 Greeks at Carbon and Emery counties' coal and coke mines;
1900–1920: 1,000 Greeks at railroad companies throughout Intermountain area.

Greek Orthodox Church
Formative Years
The influx of the large number of Greek immigrants to Salt Lake City spawned a need for a church in the city to bind them together. This was a natural progression because, next to their families, immigrants considered their church of prime importance.

Spearheading this effort was Nicholas P. Stathakos, a man who devoted much time and effort toward this worthy goal. He was one of the organizers and leaders in the establishment of the first Greek Orthodox Church in the Intermountain West.

On January 22, 1905, all Greeks in the area were called to a meeting at the Odd Fellows Building in Salt Lake City for the purpose of organizing a church.

With about 200 in attendance, the meeting was opened by Stathakos who, in a lengthy speech, pointed out the need to establish a church in Salt Lake City and cited all the benefits it would produce. He moved for the election of a twelve-member Board of Trustees that would begin receiving donations and start the search for a priest as well as undertake related duties.

Upon approval of this motion, the first Board of Trustees was elected and consisted of: Nicholas P. Stathakos, Stavros Skliris, George Soteropoulos, Konstantinos Papaioannou, Michael Litrivis, John Macheras, George Demetrakopoulos, Andreas Papanikolaou, Anastasios Papadopoulos (Pappas), Stelios Theoharis, George Christofilou, and Gregory Soteropoulos.

The board elected Stathakos president, Pappas secretary, and Skliris and Gregory Soteropoulos were directed to establish an election committee.

This board was authorized to obtain the necessary incorporation documents from the State of Utah formally establishing the church, raise funds to build a church, obtain the services of a priest, and locate a temporary place of worship while the church was built. In addition, plans were made to prepare a constitution and bylaws by which the newly organized Greek community of Utah would function.

During the winter and spring of 1905, the new community leaders did a great deal of work. A church site was selected at 439 West 400 South and the property was purchased for $1,600, payable over three years.

Bingham Canyon Main Street, 1927.

Church Ledger for February 1905

DONATIONS			EXPENSES	
Feb. 13, donation	$	90.00	Feb. 9, Metropolitan	$224.00
Feb. 24, donation	$	124.25	Feb. 9, Rent of Hall	4.00
Feb. 25, donation	$	34.00		**$228.00**
Feb. 27, donation	$	67.00		
		$315.25		

By the end of February 1905, 724 individuals had donated $1,677.75 to the church project. While one donation was for $100, two were for $25, and several for $10, most ranged from 50 cents to one dollar. Greeks living in Salt Lake City, Murray, and Bingham Canyon contributed. It is believed the $224 expense for the Metropolitan listed in that original ledger sheet represented a donation to the head of the church in Greece for the purpose of obtaining a priest.

First Priest Called

In April 1905, Archimandrite Parthenos Lymberopoulos arrived in Salt Lake City and assumed duties as the first Greek Orthodox priest for the area, sent to the fledgling parish by the Holy Synod of Greece. Soon after his arrival, plans were made for a holy liturgy to be performed in a temporary place of worship on the third floor of the Utah National Bank Building at Main Street and First South. That historic service occurred on Sunday, April 24, 1905. The Greek Orthodox Church of Salt Lake City was a reality.

With the church organized in Salt Lake City in 1905 serving as the catalyst, other Greek Orthodox church-communities came on the scene in the region: 1905 in Pueblo, Colorado; 1906 in Denver, Colorado; 1908 in McGill, Nevada; 1916 in Price, Utah; Rock Springs, Wyoming; and in Pocatello, Idaho; and in 1939–1940 in Ely, Nevada.

May was an important month as far as church administration was concerned. Three important meetings were held:

Gust Papadopoulos and his son John G. stand in front of the Collias-Papadopoulos (Pappas) Grocery at 102 South 500 West, circa 1920s.

Archimandrite Parthenos Lymberopoulos, first priest at Holy Trinity Church, 439 West 400 South, officiated at a funeral in 1908.

May 8, 1905: The Board of Trustees met in a special meeting to consider the salary of the priest, and unanimously set the pay at $80 a month, plus 25 percent of everything he collected outside the State of Utah. In other action, Nicholas Stathakos, Steve Skliris, George Christofilou, and Anastasios Pappas were appointed to draw up a constitution.

May 28, 1905: About 100 people gathered to consider a proposition to incorporate the proposed church under the name of the Greek Community of Utah. Board of Trustees President Stathakos read the proposed articles of incorporation three times (a real chore as the articles are comprised of five legal-size pages). The following quotation

ARTICLES OF INCORPORATION

OF THE

GREEK COMMUNITY OF UTAH.

5223

STATE OF UTAH,
COUNTY OF SALT LAKE, SS.

Nicholas P. Stathakes and *Ernest Pappas* do solemnly swear that at a meeting of the members of the Eastern Orthodox Greek Church, of Salt Lake City and County and various parts within the State of Utah, at which meeting *Nicholas P. Stathakes* was elected chairman and said *Ernest Pappas* was elected secretary, and held at the temporary place of worship of said members, on the third floor of the Utah National Bank Building, corner of Main and First South Streets, in Salt Lake City, Utah, on Sunday, May 28th, 1905, at 12 o'clock noon of that day, pursuant to a notice stating the time, place and object of said meeting published in the Salt Lake Tribune, a daily newspaper published at Salt Lake City, Utah, and printed in the English language and having a general circulation in the County of Salt Lake and throughout the State of Utah, said notice being published for a period of fourteen days before the time of holding said meeting and by posting

from the articles clearly indicates the dual purpose of the church-community as the founders envisioned it:

> The worship of Almighty God, instruction in religion according to the obligation and faith of the Eastern Orthodox Greek Church and to inculcate principles of good citizenship within the United States of America among the members of said organization and Greek race.

The board met immediately after the acceptance of the articles of incorporation to sign the appropriate documents. After the signing ceremony, the positions of vice president and treasurer were filled by secret ballot. Steve Skliris was elected vice president, and George Christofilou treasurer, completing the first slate of officers of the community.

As has been the case throughout the church-community's history, this founding board wrestled with expenses and income, as shown in the following ledger:

Church Ledger for May 1905

INCOME		EXPENSES	
1 Easter	$365.35	Priest's Salary	$ 80.00
1 Easter	5.55	Candles	41.75
9 Dues – Murray	76.00	Rental of hall for church	60.00
9 Donation	4.00	Title of lot	4.00
10 Dues – Murray	19.50	Room rental for priest	8.00
15 Dues & donations	16.50	Food for priest	3.35
5 Tray	11.05	Preparation of icons	15.00
6 Tray	6.90	Rental for priest	2.50
6 Dues	5.00	Newspaper ad	2.05
12 Dues – Bingham	22.40	Room for priest	1.00
16 Dues	10.00	For ticket to Bingham	1.80
21 Dues	11.50	For carriage	3.25
28 Dues	12.50	Stove and coal	4.50
Total income	**$566.25**	**Total expenses**	**$227.20**

During the summer of 1905, an intensive campaign was conducted by the community to raise funds to build a church. Archimandrite Lymberopoulos, in addition to serving the religious needs of the local group, made numerous fund-raising visits to area mining camps, railroad camps, and other pockets of Greek immigrant populations. Funds also were donated by Greeks living outside of Salt Lake City who considered the new church as their own even though they realized they would not be able to attend services regularly.

Cornerstone Laid

The culmination of the original fund-raising effort occurred on July 20, 1905, when the cornerstone of the new church was laid.

This milestone was recorded in the *Deseret Evening News* of July 21, 1905:

> The Greek community of Utah held an interesting service yesterday afternoon at the laying of the cornerstone of the Salt Lake Church. The program was not long, but included two speeches, and was witnessed by a large gathering of Greeks. The men, among whom there are no capitalists, or even well-to-do merchants, have gave [sic] more than liberally to establish a place of worship here, and the success of their cooperative effort is a matter of which they are most pleased.

> The services were entirely in the Greek language. Parthenios [sic] Lymberopoulos, who since April last has been the spiritual head of the Utah Greeks, officiated in the full robes of his office. After he had placed the stone in place, N.P. Stathakos, a prominent Greek organizer, and a man very loyal to the traditions of the Greek nation, made a fervent patriotic speech. He congratulated this community on being strong enough to support a church, and pointed to this evidence of ideals to show that the faith of the American people in the Greeks, in allowing them to enter America, and making it pleasant for them here, was not misplaced. He urged all those present to be watchful of the laws and obey them and to be true to the country they had adopted as their own, as well as true to the country from which they had come. He ended by proposing three cheers for the American people and three for the Greek people.

> The Church is located on Fourth West Street between Third and Fourth South. When completed it will accommodate about 1,500 worshippers.

The excitement of the ceremony abated as the main tasks of operating the parish took precedence, as indicated by parish financial records:

Church Ledger for August 1905

DONATIONS		EXPENSES	
Anonymous	$ 100.00	Priest's salary	$ 80.00
Misc. donations	5.00	Chanter's salary	10.00
Tray August 5	6.50	Printing charter	59.10
Tray August 14	7.60	Legal fees	10.65
Loan Walker Bros.	7000.00	Picture – church	2.00
Tray August 20	4.81	For ticket to Bingham	3.00
Sale of bonds	172.75	Contractor	450.00
Sale of bonds	285.00		750.00
Sale of bonds	190.00		800.00
Dues	15.50	Tickets Castle Gate	11.40
Sale of bonds	400.00	Cleaning of church	1.00
Tray August 27	7.45	Flowers	1.00
Tray August 28	56.50	Rent for last month	24.00
		Title of lot	4.00
Total income	**$8,251.11**	**Total expenses**	**$2,206.15**

The first funerals in the parish, in August 1905, were for Epimannondas Mitrou from Levithi, Arcadia, Greece, and for Elias Kousis from Orgolidos, Greece. The first baptisms, also in August, were for Petros, son of Mr. and Mrs. Elias Tobianebitsi, and Martha, daughter of Mr. and Mrs. Bambis Slivari.

In October, the Board of Trustees appointed Theodore Moutis and Mr. Politis to serve as chanters for the new church. Many individuals have served faithfully in this capacity during the past 100 years, and their services have added to the beauty of the liturgy of the church.

With the establishment of a dedicated leadership group, a funding system for the construction and support of a church edifice, and the services of an Orthodox priest, devoted parishioners prepared to grow their Greek church-community into a flourishing entity in the Twentieth Century.

"There were about two thousand (Greeks in Greek Town) easy and during a holiday the streets were full of Greeks. In those days there were no automobiles, just the horse-drawn beer wagons...

During the holidays and after work the streets were always full of Greeks. They had no place to meet and visit so they would line up on boths sides of the street and visit with one another."

—*Theodore Marganis, b. 1892*
Greek Oral History Collection

Mining wasn't the only enterprise in the Bingham Canyon area. This goat ranch thrived there in the early 1900s.

The George Demetriades family, shown in this portrait taken in Salt Lake City around 1913, represents a rarity in the story of Greek immigration. Maria G. Demetriades, standing third from left, came to the United States in 1898, and subsequently brought over her father, three brothers, her sister, and later, her mother Zafero Demetriades, second from left. Others in the photo are Alma Demetriades, standing left, and Helen Skedros Rizos, right. Seated are George Demetriades, left, Frosso Skedros, Alexandra Demetriades, Helen Fotis, and Marie Fotis.

Chapter 2

Dawn of the Greek Church-Community

The importance of a church edifice to act as a social and religious focal point for the Greek immigrants of the Salt Lake area cannot be fully appreciated in 2005. In 1905, the Greeks as an ethnic minority of working people had not yet established themselves as an economic business presence in the valley, nor was their culture and traditional heritage appreciated. The foresight of these early church planners and supporters to begin the overwhelming task of funding a building program, securing a priest, and organizing all aspects of sustaining sacred, social, and educational support services for their parish members remains, in retrospect, an awe-inspiring accomplishment.

Themeeting

The Board of Trustees' meeting on October 14, 1905, was pivotal for the parish as it set the tone for the new church's first service.

The new church was ready for occupancy, and it was decided to invite political leaders and other prominent Salt Lake City citizens to the first service. Stavros Skliris, Anastasios Papadopoulos, and Andreas Papanikolaou were appointed to plan a program for the ceremony. Other responsibilities were as follows: Karavelis and Macheras, ushers; Soteropoulos, collection trays; Christofilou, vigil lamps; Demetrakopoulo, candles.

The board decided to invite the Vice Consul of Greece, George Tsolomiti, living in Butte, Montana. Skliris and

Parish Board Members Present at First Service Planning Meeting

Nicholas P. Stathakos, president
Anastasios Papadopoulos, secretary
Members:
Vasilios Karavelis
George Christofilou
Gregory Soteropoulos
George Demetrakopoulos
John Macheras
Stavros Skliris
Andreas Papanikolaou

Macheras were chosen to be masters of ceremonies, but Macheras declined the offer in favor of Skliris. A committee, consisting of Stathakos, Christofilou, Soteropoulos, and Papanikolaou, was formed to decorate the church, clean the church yard, install two telephones, place the water, and obtain enough chairs for the invited officials. Date of the first church service would be October 29, 1905, and it was decided Stathakos would give a speech in Greek and chanters for the day would be Theodore Moutis and Mr. Politis.

Holy Trinity Church Consecration
The October 29, 1905 consecration services attracted Greeks from throughout the Intermountain region. Among the 1,000 in attendance were city and state dignitaries. During these ceremonies the church was named *Agia Trias* or Holy Trinity.

With their roots firmly implanted in the community, the Greeks in 1906 celebrated Greek Independence Day on March 25 for the first time in Salt Lake City. City and state dignitaries were invited to participate in this celebration honoring the heroes of the Greek War of Independence of 1821.

Look closely and you can see that the "women" on this parade float are actually men. This parade took place in Salt Lake City's "Greek Town" in 1910.

Greek History Makers

During 1907, Dr. Peter Kassinikos, a medical doctor who later served as president of the community, was appointed Greek consul by the royal Greek government. He was to serve all foreign-born Greeks in the Intermountain area.

The first wedding ceremony performed in the church was on February 9, 1907, when George Dokos and Helen Pharmakis were married, with Steve Skliris as best man.

The first American-born baby of full Greek parentage in the Salt Lake City Greek community was born in Midvale on April 13, 1907. He was James C. Dokos, son of Chris and Marina Dokos.

Unfavorable Perceptions

During the first decade of the Twentieth Century, the public (American/Salt Lake City) perception of Greek immigrants was very negative due to violence involving the Greeks and to prejudice against so-called "immoral foreigners."

May 21, 1907: At Bingham Junction (Midvale) a confrontation involving Greek and Austrian laborers led to the shooting death of Anastasios Kovallis.

May 24, 1907: The edition of the *Intermountain Republican* newspaper included a major story concerning the funeral of Kovallis that was held at the Greek Church at 439 West 400 South. According to the report, after the funeral a procession was formed with the band of the 29th Infantry Regiment from Fort Douglas in the lead. The band was followed by the casket placed on a horse-drawn carriage and by more than 400 Greeks who marched four abreast to 200 South and 500 West and then east on 200 South to State Street. There the procession boarded several carriages and streetcars that traveled to Mt. Olivet Cemetery. The purpose of this large procession by the Greeks was to emphasize that Greek immigrants had respect for Utah's laws.

November 9, 1907: In yet another unfavorable episode, the *Salt Lake Herald Republican* reported a near lynching of a Greek by a mob of 200 locals. The incident occurred at 400 West and 200 South when an American, Frank Egan, allegedly took a suitcase belonging to Bill Rodas, a Greek, who was accused of beating Egan in a fight over the suitcase. The melee attracted a large mob, including many who wanted to lynch Rodas. Fortunately for Rodas, several Greeks and Italians from the various businesses and rooming houses in the area came to his aid—as did the police—who arrested Rodas and several of his Greek and Italian backers.

"Well, I was angry when I came here. Because when I came here they (the children at Arlington school in Murray) didn't like us…The girls were very nice, really…but the boys were awfully mean. They were teasing me and used to call me 'dirty Greek' and everything else."

—*Tessie Jouflas, b. 1906*
Greek Oral History Collection

Construction of stockade cribs
at 200 South 600 West, 1908.

Greek Militia, 1910–1912.

In 1908, an unfortunate turn of events that exacerbated the negative perception of Greeks was a movement started by a Salt Lake businessman who promoted the relocation of the city's "red light" district from the downtown district. Such a move became a reality in 1908 when Salt Lake City Mayor John Bransford, with the approval of the city council, formed a real estate firm known as Citizens Investment Company, which bought most of block 64 located in the center of "Greek Town." A stockade of about 100 cribs was built there and was enclosed by a brick wall. On the evening of December 18, about 100 alleged prostitutes who were operating in the central city were sent to the stockade.

According to reports, Mayor Bransford and others picked the site because they felt the "foreign element present there" had caused the area to deteriorate. "We found that most of the better class of residents was [sic] leaving the area anyway because of the influx of Italians and Greeks who live in that neighborhood," the mayor is quoted as saying to the news media. The city leaders also rationalized that moving the prostitutes to this part of the city allegedly catered to the "immoral foreigners" residing and working there.

"I know of a time when I was going to school, they used to call me a 'dirty Greek,' and you know what happened to them? I beat the hell out of them."

—*Wilma Klekas, b. 1902*
Greek Oral History Collection

Greek-language Newspapers As the

Greek population grew in Salt Lake City, a Greek-language newspaper was needed. The first, the *Ergatis* (The Worker), 1908, was published by Peter Sioris. Following were the *Evzone*, 1910, published by G. Fotopoulos; *To Fos* (The Light), 1922, published by Peter Kassinikos, Alexander Kassinikos, Nicholas Cotro-Manes, and Ernest K. Pappas.

By the late 1920s, local Greek-language newspapers were replaced by two New York City-based broadsheets, the *Atlantis* and the *National Herald*. While doing a credible job of reporting on events pertaining to Greece and to Greek immigrants nationally, reporting of Salt Lake City news unfortunately was nonexistent. Salt Lake City Greek news often was reported in *Kalifornia*, published in San Francisco.

The Greek Militia The Greek community of

Salt Lake attracted media attention in 1910 when the so-called "Greek Militia" came on the scene.

May 2, 1910: It was reported that a "Greek Militia" had been formed. An article in the *Salt Lake Herald Republican* stated that approximately 200 Greeks were involved and uniforms were being purchased. The purpose of the group was to repel invaders of their native land. The group stated its members would obey the laws of the United States.

May 5, 1910: It was announced that Utah's governor and attorney general were investigating the "Greek Militia" to see if any state laws had been violated when it was established. The article also stated that the Utah National Guard had given its approval of the militia.

The formation of the "Greek Militia" was indicative of the strong nationalistic feelings of the Greek immigrants. Their love and devotion to the mother country was paramount and unwavering. The statement about the Greeks' "preparing to repel the invaders" was a reference to Turkey, which had ruled over Greece for nearly 400 years.

December 11, 1910: The major crisis in Greece in 1910 was the issue of Crete's desire to unite with Greece. At the conclusion of a special meeting, the leadership of the Salt Lake City Greek community sent the following telegram to the *New York Herald*, one of America's most influential newspapers of that period:

> *The Greek Community of Utah in a General Assembly specially called, resolved to express its deep gratitude to the* New York Herald *for its aid to the Cretan cause. The suggestion and offer to present Crete's cause to the Christian World for judgment, coming from a newspaper of worldwide reputation and power, is a guarantee and assurance that the struggle of centuries of a Christian race for liberty will soon be at end.*

The telegram was signed by Peter Kassinikos, president, and Ernest K. Pappas, secretary, of the community.

Several hundred Greek immigrants volunteered to fight in the Balkan War, 1912–1913. This group of volunteers was photographed in front of the Holy Trinity Church.

Highlights of the Period

In 1911, Stathakos organized a savings and loan company in Salt Lake City in which hundreds of Greek and Albanian immigrants deposited their hard-earned savings. Ironically, the man who had helped organize the first Greek Orthodox Church in the region later was found guilty of embezzling company funds.

The advent of the Balkan War in 1912–1913 saw members of the Salt Lake City Greek community answer the call of their homeland. No records are available as to the exact number that left Salt Lake City for Greece, but the *Salt Lake Herald Republican* on October 4, 1912, reported that 150 Greeks from the Bingham Canyon area had departed for Greece.

Kalifornia a Greek-language newspaper reported on October 19, 1912, that an estimated 1,500 volunteers from Utah left for Europe. Two weeks later, on November 2, the same newspaper reported that 125 Greeks left Ogden, Utah, for Greece. Most volunteers returned to America immediately after the war, many with brides and family members.

Early Clergy

Finding and employing competent clergy was a critical issue during the community's early years. With no single Greek religious authority in the United States, each local community hired and fired clergymen and this was the case in Salt Lake City.

In March 1912, the church board signed a contract to employ Fr. Germanos Papanagiotou, hired in conformity with the bylaws of the Greek community of Utah. In August, Fr. Papanagiotou was dismissed and Fr. Vasilios Lampridis was hired. As a result, a legal complaint against the board was filed in the Third Judicial District Court of Salt Lake County. Filers were John Stavrakis, Tom Politz, and John Demaras.

On September 6, the court issued a restraining order preventing the board from paying Fr. Lampridis and called for him to refrain from exercising the functions of priest of the church. The following day, the court issued a modification of its decision striking the segment refraining Fr. Lampridis from exercising his functions as a priest. Then, on September 30,

1912, the court ruled it had no jurisdiction on the subject of the actions it issued regarding the original complaint. The case was dismissed. Fr. Papanagiotou left Salt Lake City and Fr. Lampridis remained. Among other things, the complaint stated:

> Fr. Lampridis' contract had not been approved by the Greek Embassy in the U.S.; that it had not been approved by the Holy Synod of Greece, and that it did not conform with the bylaws of the Greek Community of Utah.

Hiring and firing of clergy became a volatile issue throughout the country between 1910 and 1920 because the demand for clergy was outpacing the supply. Salt Lake City was an excellent example of this dilemma as it hired eight different clergymen between 1912 and 1922. The national clergy crisis subsided somewhat once the Greek Archdiocese in New York City was organized in 1922 and parishes became better organized.

Miners on Strike

In September 1912, a major confrontation unfolded at the Utah Copper Mine in Bingham Canyon. The Western Federation of Miners that involved 4,000 workers, 1,210 of them Greeks—the largest single group of strikers—called a labor strike. The strike also involved 2,000–2,500 Greeks who worked in the mills and smelters in Murray, Midvale, Arthur, Garfield, Magna, and Tooele.

In addition to seeking increased wages and the recognition of the union, the Greeks at Utah Copper were striking to end the influence of the Greek labor agent, Leonidas Skliris. In addition to marching in picket lines, many of the striking Greek miners armed themselves and took military-type defensive positions in the hills above Bingham. This led to fears that a pitched battle would be ignited, pitting the armed strikers against deputy sheriffs and Utah National Guard troops assigned to keep the peace.

In an effort to defuse the volatile situation and to encourage the Greeks to attend a meeting with Utah's Governor William Spry, Fr. Vasilios Lampridis, the Greek Orthodox priest from Salt Lake City, walked up the mountain to the Greek strikers. The *Salt Lake Tribune*, September 20, 1912, described what took place:

> Their warlike spirit [was] subdued temporarily by a lone priest of the Greek Church, Father Vasilios Lambrides, [sic] who exhorted them in the name of their religion to refrain from further violence and defiance of the law.
>
> The little father dressed in flowing clerical robes with a glittering cross of gold upon his breast, went among the militant strikers like the spirit of peace and brought "the truce of God." Everywhere guns were laid aside for him and hats were doffed in respectful salute.
>
> With few exceptions the men left their trenches and trooped down to the meeting place where Governor Spry was waiting to address them.

In a related event, Ernest K. Pappas, a leader and spokesman for the Greek community as well as the striking Greek workers, wrote a letter that concerned the activities of labor boss Leonidas Skliris, which was published:

> This padrone has grown rich on his exploitation of Greek laborers whom he had induced to come to California, Utah, Nevada and Colorado by advertising in all Greek newspapers in the United States. These newspapers are widely circulated in Greece and Crete. On arrival these immigrants pay Skliris or his underlings $5 to $20 or more. This applies not only to Bingham Canyon, but coalmines at Castle Gate, Kenilworth, Helper, Sunnyside, Scofield, etc.
>
> The Greeks would not have left the mines had the padrone system not been in effect.
>
> As to the grocery store charge, it is well known that Steve G. Skliris, Leon G. Skliris' representative, approves every Greek hired by Utah Copper and threatens with dismissal those who do not trade at Pan Hellenic. The threats go farther by saying, "Your account this month is too small. You've been buying elsewhere. We look out for your job, you look out for us." If Greeks are loyal, why did they join union head first, 700 in one night took oath to gain freedom from the padrone system.
>
> —*Deseret Evening News*
> *September 22, 1912*

Two days later, on September 24, 1912, Skliris resigned as the labor agent for Utah Copper. The Greek miners were exuberant over this action as it marked the end of the despised "padrone system" at the work sites.

Clergy: 1905–1926

Archimandrite Parthenos
   Lymberopoulos, 1905–1912
The Rev. Germanos
   Papanagiotou, 1912
The Rev. Vasilios Lampridis,
   1912–1913
Archimandrite Dorotheos
   Bourazanis, 1913–1916
The Rev. Ambrosios
   Mandilaris, 1916–1917
The Rev. Nicholas Patsulis,
   1917–1918
The Rev. Christos
   Angelopoulos, 1918–1921
The Rev. Athanasios Tsiamis,
   1921–1922
The Rev. John Aivaliotis, 1922
Archimandrite Bartholomeos
   Karahalios, 1922–1926

As the strike continued, the *Salt Lake Tribune* reported, on September 22, 1912: "...800 Cretans had been shipped into Utah from the coast and other points as strike breakers."

On October 11, 1912, the newspaper reported "A mass meeting was held by a large number of Greeks in Salt Lake City at the Greek Orthodox Church where they drafted a protest letter to the Greek Consul in Washington D.C., protesting the harsh treatment of the Greek strikers."

Greek Schools

Growing up in two different cultures—Greek at home and American (English language) outside the home—was a challenge for the young generation. They were members of families with strong ties to the Orthodox Church, the Greek language, and its culture, but they were American-born and were exposed daily to American influence.

The need to pass on to subsequent generations the importance of perpetuating the Greek language, the Orthodox religion, and the culture and traditions rooted in the "mother country" was very important to the early Greek families, as well as to later generations.

The Board of Trustees created the first Greek-language school (Greek school) committee in 1915. Its primary function was to spearhead financial support for the Greek school in Salt Lake but it also served as the catalyst for other Greek schools organized in areas outside Salt Lake City.

The first Greek school was organized later that year with James Demetriadis (Demas) serving as its first teacher. In 1920, the school was located in the Ness Building on 200 South between Main Street and West Temple. The primary curriculum was based upon basic learning of Greek—reading and writing. Since Greek was the language spoken at home, the children were able to converse fluently in Greek. Attendance was mandatory, parents were very supportive of the school and a student missing school or misbehaving was not tolerated. In addition to the basics of reading, writing, and grammar, the students participated in Greek Independence Day observances, often dressed in authentic costumes while they recited poems, sang patriotic songs in Greek, and participated in stage productions.

Attending Greek school was not the most desirable thing for the young people, especially those in higher grades. It was difficult to devote time to Greek school and also find time for other schoolwork, possible part-time employment, and participation in public school activities. Later, many second-generation Greek Americans recalled disdain for attending Greek school. At the same time, they were grateful to be able to read, write, and speak Greek, especially as they grew older and learned to appreciate their language and culture. During the early years of the school program, educational materials were scarce, but through the efforts of the few well-educated teachers available, the school functioned quite effectively.

Tony Bobolis posed in Ogden, Utah, circa 1910, in a native Greek costume.

Greek school class, 1925. Teachers Angeline Skedros, left, Dorothy Katris, right; men standing, James Velis, left, Steve Pappas, Archimandrite Barthalomeos Karahalios, and Mr. Pikoulas, were members of Greek school committee.

Later, in the years following 1960, well-prepared educational materials became available from various sources.

Between the 1920s and the 1930s, several new teachers were added, including Angeline Skedros, who was a graduate of a teacher-training college in Greece, John Zaharogianis, Katina Demiris, and Helen Halori.

In the late 1920s, Greek schools also flourished in Magna and Bingham Canyon, followed by schools in Tooele, Ogden, Midvale, Layton, and West Jordan. By 1925, the Salt Lake Greek school was located in the lower level of the newly built

"I think mother had a real sad life primarily because she'd lost her two husbands in the mines and she grieved all her life, her whole life 'til the day she died. She wore black for forty years. She didn't go out and celebrate. She wouldn't even go to a movie for years and years. She just deprived herself of any type of social function. She just didn't feel like she should do it. As the years went by, we changed her a little. We got her to where she wore something besides cotton black hose and cotton black dresses and something that was a little dressier. But not much.

—Andy Katsanevas, b. 1922
Greek Oral History Collection

Holy Trinity Church, with classes being held Monday through Friday between 4:30 p.m. and 6:30 p.m.

In the mid-1930s, Greek classes were held at the now-razed Fremont School at 200 West (now 300 West) between 200 and 100 South Streets. During the early 1940s, Greek classes were held at the Oquirrh Elementary School on 400 East between 300 and 400 South Streets.

Greek school was a "must" for children of Greek Immigrants. This large class, circa 1934, was taught by Helen Halori, standing left, second row down, and Katina Demiris, far right. The men, Pantelis Marinakis, top row left, William Souvall, top center and George Foundas, right, were members of the Greek School Committee.

Teachers who served between 1915–1975:

Mary Benakis	Fr. Antonios Kalogeropoulos
Elaine Bovos	John Klekas
William D. Cocorinis	James Louvaris
Mrs. Gus Cutrubis	Aphrodite Marcooles
Jenny Davis	Constantine Milenopoulos
James Demas	Fr. George Politis
Katina Demiris	Helen Praggastis
Panos Doudaniotis	Ernest Praggastis
James C. Dokos	Angeline Skedros
Artemios Efthimiathes	Rev. Fr. Artemios Stamatiadis
Peter Gianopoulos	Mary Varanakis
Helen Halori	Antonios Voyazis
Dorothy Katris	John Zaharogianis
Ourania Kalogeropoulos	Penelope Zolas

Greek school classes since the 1970s have been conducted at Holy Trinity Cathedral and Prophet Elias Church in Holladay.

Greek classes extended well beyond the local Greek community in September 1948. Through the efforts of the Hellenic Improvement Association and Dr. Jacob Geerlings, professor of classical Greek at the University of Utah, a Modern Greek class was offered at the university. Greek immigrant William D. Cocorinis was its first instructor, a position he held until his death in 2003.

1916–1917 Political Crisis in Greece

In 1916–1917, Allied forces occupied Salonika, Greece, and the country eventually entered the war on the side of the Allied nations. In 1919, Eleftherios Venizelos represented Greece at the Paris Peace Conference. That was followed by a change of political leadership in Greece in 1920 that saw the return of the royalist faction to power.

In the United States, the chaotic and constantly changing political situation in Greece during 1913–1922 had seriously divided many Greek communities along royalist and anti-royalist lines. Indicative of the split in loyalties, in 1921 two competing archbishops, each representing a major political faction in Greece, were sent to the United States.

Greek Politics Cause Fight in Coffee House

"…I went to school at age five and then after that I got so I could interpret for my mother whenever, you know, the situation came up and the neighbors would come visit her because she was a marvelous cook and very hospitable. And so we had Mrs. Kroh and Mrs. Pitts…and then of course her Greek ladies. She was very excited when they came because she could visit with them, but when the others came she would just sit there and then they would talk and I would tell my mother what they'd say…you know, usually when your peers came to visit you, your children don't stick around, but we had to because we served as interpreters."

—Ellen V. Furgis, b. 1926
Greek Oral History Collection

The Greek community of Salt Lake City in 1916–1917 also became involved in the political crisis in Greece. As a result, the anti-royalists group organized a temporary community, brought in a priest, and held regular church services in a temporary church at 200 South and West Temple.

On January 4, 1917, the *Salt Lake Herald Republican* reported that threats had been made against Fr. S. M. Vasilas of the newly organized anti-royalist Greek Orthodox Church in Salt Lake City. Ernest Pappas, one of the leaders of the new group, said that the threats were unfounded. A committee consisting of Fr. Vasilas, Ernest Pappas, George Castles, Frank Kyriopoulos, and George Cozakos visited the newsroom of the *Herald* to protest the story. Evidently another priest, Fr. Nicholas Patsulis, had also served the anti-royalist group. Fr. Patsulis also served the Holy Trinity Church group.

On February 12, 1917, the *Salt Lake Herald Republican* reported that a "reunion" of the Greek Orthodox Holy Trinity group and the newly formed anti-royalist group would be considered by both groups at a special meeting the following week. Fr. Ambrosios Mandilaris, who spoke excellent English, was the pastor of the Holy Trinity Church. According to the article, Fr. Mandelaris hoped to see Fr. Vasilas remain as his assistant.

Church records show that in 1917 a special committee was appointed by the general assembly to reunite the Greek community until regular elections could be held. The members of this important committee, credited with bringing peace and unity to the Greek community, were Peter E. Athas, William Vasilacopoulos, George Kyrinakos, William Kanelopoulos, John George, George Castles, and Ernest K. Pappas. Shortly thereafter, a regularly elected Board of Trustees took the helm of the church and a new priest, Fr. Christos Angelopoulos, arrived on the scene. The Greek community was again united under his leadership.

Other 1917 Happenings

April 10: The Salt Lake Greek Orthodox Church instituted the practice of raising funds by the use of solicitation trays at church functions in hopes of obtaining financial support of the Greek-language school. The trays were first passed in church on Sunday, April 10. Previously, this fund-raising method was used to collect funds in support of the Royal Greek Navy.

August 15: The first community picnic was held, inaugurating a practice observed annually until 1969. When the Prophet Elias Greek Orthodox Church was opened in the southeastern suburbs of Salt Lake City in December 1969, it was decided that the annual community gathering would be held on the Sunday prior to or immediately after Prophet Elias' name day, at the picnic grounds of Prophet Elias. In the 1950s, community picnics also were held at Lagoon, an amusement park midway between Salt Lake City and Ogden.

• A murder in Salt Lake City's "Greek Town" in June of 1917 shocked the community at the very time it was attempting to project a favorable image. The *Herald Republican* of June 28, reported the incident this way: "...*in what was characterized by the Salt Lake police as an open attempt by an afternoon newspaper to incite friends of Bruce Dempsey, 16 year-old brother of boxer Jack Dempsey, young Dempsy was killed by Peter Terloupis, a Greek immigrant, nearly resulting in a mob lynching.*"

Indeed, a lynching nearly occurred in front of the Salt Lake City police station on 100 South and State Streets. A large crowd gathered there, hoping to force its way into the county jail where Terloupis was being held. He had been captured, while hiding in a Layton farmhouse, by a posse led by William Cayias, a Greek deputy sheriff.

Pappas Wins Again

Andrew Pappas was re-elected president of the Greek community for his fourth term of two years at the electon in the Greek colony held Sunday. There was no friction in the meeting and members of the community for the most part voted the straight ticket headed by Mr. Pappas. In addition twelve trustees of the community who will administer the affairs of the Greek Catholic Orthodox Church for the coming two years were elected. The trustees are James Kolonelos, John Papavasiliou, Nick Theodorelos, Peter Kouvavas, John Lymberis, E. Karabatos, James Lambros, Peter Pharmakis, Gus Makris, Andrew Savas and Thomas Spanos. Four of the trustees are from Salt Lake, one from Murray, one from Midvale, two from Pleasant Green and Garfield, two from Bingham and one from Tooele.

There were more than 1,200 ballots cast in the election and those in charge of the balloting declared if the weather had been good that there would have been more than 2,000 votes cast. The polls were open the entire day after morning services in the Greek Church. More than 100 Greeks came from Bingham after 4 o'clock p.m. They hired all of the automobiles and stages in that place to get here for the election.

The campaign made for Mr. Pappas was one of the quietest that has been conducted in the Greek colony for a number of years. He did not have any opposition when the time came for nominating candidates, as the faction which opposed him before nominations were made refused to put a ticket in the field.

Ernest Lolos, one of the leading members of the Greek community, in a statement last night declared that the Greeks desired to unanimously elect Mr. Pappas for the work he has done during the past six years. Mr. Lolos said Mr. Pappas has done more for the Greek people than any other member of the community, and that the protection he gave the Greek immigrant had strengthened sentiment for him. In addition to being president of the Greek community, Mr. Pappas represents the Greek government in Utah.

—*Herald Republican*
December 11, 1916

Andrew Pappas, highly respected, served eight years as Greek community president.

World War I Era With the declaration of war between the United States and Germany in 1917, the Greek community of Utah purchased a $1,000 Liberty War Bond to show its support for the war effort. In addition, the first community donation of $300 was made to the American Red Cross.

During the course of the war, more than 300 Greeks volunteered or were inducted into the United States Armed Forces. The following made the supreme sacrifice for their adopted country:

James Anagnostakis   *Bill Kallas*
George N. Bernardis   *Demetrios Karvarites*
James Dacolias   *Theros Kechepolas*
John Doles   *Louis Monas*
Evangelos Fintrilakis   *George Palioudakis*
William Gatsakos (Jackson)   *Constantine D. Papademetriou*
Bill Georgopoulos   *James J. Wallas*
Theodore E. Gooras

Greek immigrants who did not enter the armed forces during the war supported the effort by purchasing Liberty Bonds and by working in the critical mining industries of the state. A well educated and respected member of the community, Maria G. Demetriades, was instrumental in selling war bonds with patriotic fervor, encouraging her fellow Greeks to help finance the war effort.

June 28, 1918: The *Herald Republican* reported a major celebration took place in the Greek community, which was observing the first anniversary of Greece's entry into World War I on the side of the Allied nations. The events included a parade through downtown Salt Lake City and special services at the church. Principal speakers were Utah's Governor Simon Bamberger and Salt Lake City Mayor Mont Ferry.

The *Herald Republican* reported on December 30, 1918, a meeting of more than 1,500 Greeks from the greater Salt Lake City area was held the day before at the Salt Lake Theater on 100 South and State Street. Before the meeting, a parade of numerous Greeks carrying flags of the United States and Greece, led by the Greek priest and Greek-American veterans in khaki uniforms, marched in the downtown area. The purpose of the parade and related mass meeting was to publicize passage of a resolution that was to be sent to President Woodrow Wilson asking the United States to safeguard Greeks living in Bulgaria and Turkey. Peter S. Marthakis, George Photos, editor of the Greek newspaper in Salt Lake City, and John George made speeches.

The end of the First World War opened the door of opportunity for Greeks to devote themselves more fully to more resourceful community-expansion efforts.

The newly organized Pan Cretan Minos Society celebrated the end of World War I in Bingham Canyon, November 1918. John Leventis stands in front, at center of poster of U.S. President Woodrow Wilson and Greek Prime Minister Eleftherios Venizelos. Spero Vidalakis stands at left, holding American Flag.

The cornerstone for the new Holy Trinity Church was laid in 1923. Peter S. Marthakis, left, Salt Lake City Mayor Clarence C. Nelsen, Utah Governor Charles Mabey, Archimandrite Barthalomeos Karahalios, and parishioners Ernest K. Pappas, John G. Condas, and James Lambrakos were among dignitaries.

Chapter 3

Era of Expansion

*With World War I ended and peace and prosperity prevailing in America,
the community's 1915 discussion about a new church became a priority again in 1919.
A committee consisting of John George, Peter E. Athas, G. Hadtzis, George Kyrinakos,
K. Thalasohoris, Sam Collias, George Castles, and Ernest K. Pappas was appointed
by the general assembly and instructed to proceed with the sale of the
present church site and to acquire a location for a new church.*

In July 1920, the committee negotiated the sale of the Greek Church, built in 1905, to the Denver & Rio Grande Railroad Company for $18,000. The agreement allowed the community to use the facility until the new church was completed.

At the same time, the community had a committee negotiate the purchase of a new church site at 200 West (now 300 West) and 300 South. This property was bought from the Sweet Candy Company for $20,250.

A committee, appointed to raise funds for the new building, consisted of John G. Condas, Sam Kounalis, William Cayias, William Vasilacopulos, George N. Strike, James

Lambros, John Kerikas, Odysseus Pappaspirides, Peter E. Athas, Gregory Halles, William Kanelopoulos, Ernest K. Pappas, Nick Kalofon, Sam Collias, and Peter Tasoulis.

One fund-raising method was selling coupons—representing bricks—to members of the community with the coupons payable over a period of time. The Greek business community donated other funds, but the greatest support came from the families of numerous blue-collar workers and countless single men.

All the fund-raising efforts notwithstanding, the community was faced with the problem of financing the new project. At first, it was believed that a suitable church could

John S. Bogris owned the Utah Café, 40 South Main Street, in the 1920s and 1930s.

be constructed for a cost of $65,000. This figure was revised several times as various changes were made in the building plans. At a special meeting on May 20, 1923, the Board of Trustees and the building committee were given "…power and authority to negotiate a loan or loans not exceeding $40,000."

On March 20, 1924, the church received a loan from the Zions Savings Bank and Trust Company of Salt Lake City for $25,000. Terms of the loan contract stated that the amount was to be repaid during a five-year period. In addition to the mortgage, the Greek community was required to place a $25,000 bond with the bank. This bond was negotiated through the bonding company of Ashton-Jenkins of Salt Lake City. Unfortunately, a detailed financial report of the building of Holy Trinity Church (1923–1925) is not available. Other than the minutes of the Board of Trustees, no financial records or listings of donors have been found.

With the financial arrangements made, construction of the new edifice came under the supervision of the church building committee headed by its first president, Stylian Staes, the Greek Vice Consul of Salt Lake City. When Staes moved to Price, Peter S. Marthakis was appointed committee president. Other committee members were John G. Condas, vice president; John E. Kerikas, secretary; Peter E. Athas, treasurer; and Sam Collias.

The new church's cornerstone was put in place on Sunday, August 28, 1923. Attending these ceremonies were

Helen and Wilma Fotis posed in Greek dress for this 1924 photo.

Utah's Governor Charles Mabey, Salt Lake City Mayor Clarence C. Nelsen, and many other civic dignitaries. During this memorable day, several thousand dollars were collected for the new church, thanks to the generosity of major contributors: Pan Cretan Association, $2,100; George N. Strike, $850; Chris Furgis, $700; John G. Condas, $600; William Souvall, $510; Nick Floor, $525; and William Rodogiannis, $500. The total donated for the church construction from the July 15 ground-breaking activity to the cornerstone-laying activity was more than $7,500.

The events of August 28, 1923 were well covered by the newspapers:

Governor Charles Mabey and Mayor Clarence Neslen [sic] laid the cornerstones of the Trinity Cathedral at the Greek Orthodox Church to be built at Second West and Third South. Both the Governor and the Mayor with Judge M.L. Ritchie of the 3rd Judicial District Court spoke at the ceremonies. Also attending were the following guests: Former Governor Simon Bamberger, City Commissioners A.F. Barnes, and T. T. Burton. Also in attendance was Chief of Police J.E. Burbidge.

—*Deseret News*
August 28, 1923

Construction of the church started on November 20, 1923. With work progressing on schedule, it was decided to hold the first Divine Liturgy and the consecration ceremonies in the new church on August 2, 1925.

Archbishop Alexander, of New York City, fourth from left in front row, led the consecration services for the new Holy Trinity Church on August 2, 1925.

Governor Mabey spoke and said "that the building is evidence that the Greek residents of Utah intend to make their home here and to assist in the upbuilding of the community. We are going to work together." The ceremonies began with a parade from the old Holy Trinity Church at 439 South 400 West. A large crowd participated in the parade. Over 700 people were present during the ceremony. The cost of the new edifice is estimated at $100,000–$150,000. Members of the Greek Community included P. S. Marthakis, Chairman of the event, John George, past president who spoke on behalf of the Greek Community expressing the sincere appreciation and hospitality shown to the Greek Community. Other members of the committee included: Rev. Karahalios, George N. Strike, John G. Condos, Peter E. Athas and William Cayias.

—*Salt Lake Tribune*
August 28, 1923

Members of Holy Trinity Church Board of Trustees in 1924 included Bill Karapanos, back left, Nick Kasambas, James Mavrakis, Phillip Drandakis, front left, James Lambros, Odysseus Pappaspiridis, and Nicholas Melis.

with a distinctive example of Byzantine-style architecture. It also marked the fulfillment of a dream that was in the minds and hearts of all the pioneer Greek immigrants from the day they arrived in the Salt Lake Valley.

The new church and property were valued at approximately $125,000–$150,000 at the time of its opening. It has continuously served the spiritual, educational, and social needs of the dynamic and growing greater Salt Lake City church-community since that time.

Greek Community Life, 1924–1930

Salt Lake City Mayor Clarence Nelsen issued a formal invitation to former Greek Premier Venizelos, currently vacationing in Santa Barbara, California, to visit Salt Lake City. The Mayor stated that our large Greek community is well respected.

—Salt Lake Tribune
December 3, 1924

Articles of Incorporation were filed with the Secretary of State office in Salt Lake City by a newly formed organization, "Greek Americanization Club." The purpose of this group is to "foster love for our country on the part of American citizens of Greek nativity or descent and loyalty to the constitution and laws of the United States—to encourage people [of] Grecian origin in becoming American Citizens of the United States." Officers of the group: Constantine N. Antones, P. S. Marthakis, Ernest G. Mantes, Sam J. Gianos, and Anastasios Anastasopoulos.

—Salt Lake Telegram
January 25, 1925

Among the throng attending this holy service was Archbishop Alexander, the leading religious leader of the Greek Orthodox Church Archdiocese, numerous other Greek Orthodox clergy, as well as several state, city, and civic dignitaries.

The new church was named Holy Trinity, thus continuing the name of the original church built in 1905. Serving the Greek community during this period was Archimandrite Barthalomeos Karahalios.

The new Holy Trinity Church was unique in that it provided Salt Lake City and the entire Intermountain West

Winners of the 1928 oratorical contest in the Greek Community, sponsored by the Hellenic Post No. 40 of the American Legion on George Washington's birthday, are shown here: George Comarell, standing left, Margaret Stavropoulos, James C. Dokos; Helen Papadopoulos, seated left, George J. Condas, and Viola Kerikas.

Margaret Stavropoulos and George Comarell, students at West High School, won gold medals presented by the Hellenic Post Number 40 of the American Legion in the George Washington Oratorical Contest. The event took place at the Greek Orthodox Church where more than 1,000 attended. In addition to the two winners, many others were honored with silver medals and letters of commendation. They included: Anastasia Axiadaktilou, George J. Condas, Demetrios C. Dokos, Athena Takis, Constantinos G. Flogeras, Wilma Fotis, Mary J. Kerikas, Viola Kerikas, Frank Magdalin, James Nakos, Ethel Nikolas, George A. Pappas, Ellen G. Papadopoulos, Stella Pantelakis, Vasiliki Pikoulas and Theodore Speropoulos.

—Salt Lake Tribune
February 23, 1928

October 10, 1928: Apostolos Borovilos, Constantine Nickolaou, and James C. Skedros petitioned the Archdiocese, requesting that they be ordained as clergy in the Greek Orthodox Church. The petition was denied; no explanation was given. Many years later, the Archdiocese ordained laymen to the clergy—among them was Salt Lake City clergyman Fr. George Politis in 1972.

December 28, 1929: The "Holy Trinity Bell" was installed in the north bell tower of Holy Trinity Church. This effort was spearheaded by donors from Bingham Canyon: Louis Tsinakis, Stratis G. Falekakis, George C. Roumpos, Elias G. Kondodimas, and Gust G. Karpakis.

The Great Depression

The depression years, from 1929 to 1936, impacted all phases of life and placed hardships on the Salt Lake Greek Church community. In order to meet the church's expenses for basic activities and to keep it operating, unnecessary expenses were cut.

Many Greeks suffered economic losses when they were forced to close their business establishments. Others became unemployed or were forced to work on a part-time basis. Church membership dwindled to a low of 50 members in good standing—that is, paid membership. Church dues were $6 per year.

The choir and athletic clubs were popular during the economic downturn, since a shortage of funds prevented the board from supporting other youth activities. During this period John George was appointed as official lecturer of the church. He presented a series of lectures on the Orthodox church and the Greek Orthodox community to various interested Salt Lake community groups.

Despite the severe economic conditions, community progress was carried forth by dedicated members of the Boards of Trustees and the clergy, who implemented a number of progressive changes in the administration of the church. Many of these innovations were to have far-reaching consequences for years to come.

The first choir of Holy Trinity Church is shown here in 1935. Community president John Kotsovos, standing left, with chanter-director C. Milonopoulos and Fr. Harry Gavalas in the center. Choir members included: Stella Pantelakis, Angie Ligdas, Helen Arkoudas, Bessie Kosta, Kay Zekas, Helen Kerikas, Viola Kerikas, Sophie Grillos, Stella Sergakis, Josephine Zeese, Deno Kosta, James Skedros, Christine Ligdas, Sophie Gavalas, Virginia Kanell, Con Vasilacopoulos, Kay Strike, Zeffi Pappas, Lula Zeese, Katherine Coucourakis, Mary Athas, and Sophie Zeese.

Milestone Events, 1928–1936

• The Salt Lake church showed a great deal of interest in the newly organized Greek Archdiocese of North and South America, located in New York City. The constitution and bylaws of the Archdiocese were reviewed by the local membership, but no formal action was taken on this important issue. The matter of sending a church representative to the Clergy-Laity Congress of the Archdiocese was discussed, but no action was taken.

• Next to the Greek Orthodox community of Salt Lake City, the Serbian Orthodox community was the largest. In about 1910 and subsequently, a Serbian Orthodox Church was organized in Midvale. Because of internal problems, the economic depression of the 1930s, and its inability to meet expenses, the church was closed. As a result, the Greek community encouraged Serbians to become members of the Greek Orthodox Church. For many years, the Salt Lake Greek Orthodox Church continued to serve members of the various Eastern Orthodox jurisdictions in the area.

• Improvements were made to the exterior and interior of the church building. Pews were purchased, a new furnace was installed, and the church was painted.

• "Aeschylus," one of several theatrical groups, was formed in the early 1930s. The stage plays performed were spoken in Greek and usually pertained to the years of the Greek Revolution. Other performances, namely dramas and comedies, were about matters more contemporary. Such events, held on the lower level of Holy Trinity Church, usually were fund-raising activities for the benefit of the Greek school program. These amateur theatrical groups provided an outstanding source of entertainment and culture revival in the dark years of the Great Depression.

Some of the participants were:

Gust J. Anton

Paul Borovilos

Peter Cairo

Katherine Coucourakis

Katina Demiris

James Demas

Athena Demas

Bill G. Dokos

Jim C. Dokos

George C. Dokos

Napoleon C. Dokos

George N. Floor

Triantafilos Gouvisis

Louisa Kargas

Harry Kambouris

Demetra Kambouris

Deno Kosta

John Kotsovos

Panteles Marinakis

Helen G. Pappas

Gus Papacostas

Helen Papacostas

Helen S. Pappas

Andy Sakelariou

Louisa Sakelariou

James C. Skedros

Mary Skurtaniotis

Gus Sileventis

Sam W. Souvall

Andy Takis

Athena Takis

Diana Takis

Maria Takis

Tasia Vasilacopoulos

Con Vasilacopoulos

John Zaharogianis

Catherine Zaharogianis

Rozalia Zaharias

Bill Zorbas

Sylvia Zorbas

• A group called the Greek Evangelical Church was organized in Salt Lake City during the late 1920s and early 1930s. Leaders of this movement were Constantine Nickolaou and George Christopoulos. Its place of worship was on 200 East between 500 South and 600 South. In its formative

Several Greek theatrical groups provided entertainment during the 1930s. Thespians identified here are John Kotsovos, seated left, Louisa Kargas, Stamatina Arkoudas; Triantafilos Gouvisis, standing left, Paul Borovilos, and Gus Papacostas.

"...well, the Ku Klux Klan...I was at Bingham once and...they have a little trouble up there with the Greeks...Take and burn the cross out the street. That's all. He don't hurt anybody, don't kill anybody. but, uh, he don't like us anyhow. The Ku Klux Klan."

—James Korobas, b. 1891
Greek Oral History Collection

period, the new church attracted several families that regularly attended services at Holy Trinity. Most eventually returned to services at Holy Trinity Church. By the late 1970s, the Greek Evangelical Church no longer existed.

———————

Salt Lake West High mathematics teacher, Peter S. Marthakis, was recently honored by educational groups for his achievements. Mr. Marthakis came to Utah in 1904 at the age of 12 to join his father. He attended West High School and later played football for the University of Utah where he received his Bachelor of Arts degree in 1914 and Master of Arts degree in 1916 in mathematics. For the past several years he has attended summer school in California, working on his doctorate. He is a veteran of World War I, very active in the Greek community and is highly respected in educational circles.

—Salt Lake Tribune
July 13, 1931

Fire destroyed the Royal Candy Factory and the Copper King Pool Hall in Bingham. Damages are estimated at $9,000. Owners of the Royal Candy Co. are Gus Drossos and Gus Pitchios.

—Deseret News
May 6, 1931

"*Many times during the war and 1933 and 1934 we had the Ku Klux Klan. They would come—our farm was just below the Magna cemetery and the Ku Klux Klan would come above the cemetery and burn crosses, race, make noise, run around with sheets and scare everybody. They were against the Greeks, the Italians. It was just a little clan. It was the hardware man, the doctor, the drug store, just the businessmen.*"

—Wilma Klekas, b. 1902
Greek Oral History Collection

N.J. Cotro-Manes, Salt Lake City attorney, is the new commander of Hellenic Post #40 of the American Legion. Other officers are James Cozakos, first vice commander; Theodore Marganis, second vice commander; James C. Skedros, adjustant [sic]; John K. Praggastis, treasurer; George Koucas, chaplain, and Mike Koucklis, sergeant at arms.

—Salt Lake Tribune
September 17, 1932

Ninety-five children of the local Greek community are acquiring knowledge of the language, culture, and literature of their mother country. School meets at the Fremont School between 4:30-6:30 five days a week. Teachers are Fr. Artemios Stamatiadis, James Demetriadis, and Catherine Demiris. Fr. Stamatiadis said "our people believe in the public schools for English, but should also be educated in their native language."

—Salt Lake Tribune
October 13, 1933

District 30 of the Order of AHEPA (American Hellenic Educational and Progressive Association) is holding its yearly convention in Salt Lake. Attending are several hundred delegates from chapters in Utah, Idaho, Nevada, and Wyoming. The organization is composed of American citizens of Greek descent and has 300 chapters and 35,000 members in the United States. Plans were discussed for relief programs to be carried on by the various chapters. The delegates also passed a resolution to oppose radicalism to overthrow the government by force or destroy existing institutions. Local AHEPA leaders in charge of the convention include: P.S. Marthakis, past national vice president; Tom Politz, Sam Kounalis, N.J. Cotro-Manes, Harry Metos and Chris Athas.

—Salt Lake Tribune
June 1, 1934

Greeks enthusiastically attended fraternal picnics such as this one held by District 30 Order of AHEPA in City Creek Canyon in 1932.

Approximately 175 members of the National Pancretan Association met in Salt Lake this week. This is the organization's fourth national convention. The national group, which consists of former residents of Crete and their descendants, is a patriotic brotherhood. Local president of the Minos Pancretan chapter is Nicholas Mouskondis with Sam Kounalis serving as secretary.

—*Deseret News*
June 6, 1934

Note: Pancretan, as in the news article above, is also referred to in its original, traditional form Pan Cretan.

"I was blasting (dynamite charges in the copper mines near Salt lake City). It was a hard job. I blasted three times a day. And you're only supposed to blast one time a shift in those days (1911). I had one fellow (boss) named Walker. He was a son of a gun. He liked me, but by god, he killed me to work. It was better than the work on the railroad at Wendover. There I worked 10 hours a shift for $1.60."

—*Mike Bapis, b. 1894*
Greek Oral History Collection

Success Market #5 was opened at 45 East Broadway and is the largest and most complete grocery store ever built in Utah. An outstanding feature is the large revolving neon sign in the front of the building. The store includes a complete meat department, delicatessen, grocery and produce, tea room, lunch counter, cigar stand and photo shop. The new store is under the management of George Zeese and John Gerendas, owners of Success Market Co.

—Salt Lake Tribune
November 17, 1934

Fraternal Groups Emerge The Greek

immigrants not only organized communities and built religious edifices, but also organized fraternal, provincial, and national organizations.

Being gregarious by nature, Greeks flocked to these groups that provided social interaction within, and also helped marshal parishioners to participate in various church-community activities. Some of these groups are active today and, whether church-affiliated or not, they contribute significantly to the outreach of the Greek community within Utah and beyond.

While all the groups organized by the early Greeks are too numerous to list here, those that follow are some of the more prominent organizations that set the tone of mutual caring and preservation of cultural ideals.

George Zeese, founder of Success Markets, 1930–1955.

Vyzas Society members, Copperfield and Bingham Canyon, 1918.

Cultural Organizations

The Pan Hellenic National Union, the first national group, was organized in 1908, with the purpose of uniting all local Greek societies in America, but it had disappeared by 1920 because of internal politics. Several Pan Hellenic chapters that had been formed locally met the same fate.

1915: The Vyzas Society of Megara, Greece, the first Greek fraternal organization in Utah was founded in Bingham Canyon. After it disbanded locally in 1980, Vyzas was reincarnated in Queens, New York, where it is still active.

48

Salt Lake Theater Manager Gladdens the Hearts of Hospitalized Youngsters with Toys

Three Happy Youngsters and Their Benefactor

Movie Employe Plays Santa Sub To 800 Children

Party Given at Theater by Dan Kostopulos; Saves Funds From Wages

Dan Kostopulos, whose overflowing generosity as a sub for Santa brings Christmas joy to hundreds each year, Tuesday morning greeted 800 little guests at the Broadway theater in his annual sub for Santa party. These kiddies, taken from the lists of the sub for Santa department of The Salt Lake Tribune-Telegram, were given the treat of their young lives and left the theater filled with candy and lugging toys that will brighten their Christmas day.

During the past seven years, Mr. Kostopulos has devoted a major portion of his time to charities of various natures. More than 10,000 persons have been the recipients of his whole-hearted offers of assistance. Although he is active the year around, it is at Christmas that Mr. Kostopulos performs his most noteworthy service.

As a penniless immigrant 14 years ago, Mr. Kostopulos knows what it means to be a youngster and not have the things that mean everything to such a child. So he has vowed that so far as he can prevent it, no child will meet Christmas without toys. Caring for 800 children would be a major job for a person of even robust income. To Mr. Kostopulos it is a real sacrifice which, he hastens to say, he is only too happy to make. He is an employe at the Broadway theater. Surplus from his salary he conserves to bring this Christmas joy. He owns no car, uses no tobacco nor intoxicants and refrains from extravagant pleasures. As a result, he builds this sub for Santa fund.

His Christmas party Tuesday included showing of a short screen feature, a comedy cartoon, then presentation of toys and candy to each guest. This year he is also providing gifts for patients at the L. D. S. Children's hospital and the Shriner's hospital. The Utah Light & Traction company provided free transportation for the kiddies to and from the theater.

Letters and telegrams from all parts of the United States have lauded his efforts, but his most appreciated thanks are the beaming faces of the youngsters to whom his gifts are given.

Dan Kostopulos, above, with three happy youngsters from the crowd of 800 he entertained Tuesday morning in his role as Sub for Santa.

Mr. Kostopulos feted his little guests at a motion picture show and gave each toys and candy so that they could have a complete Christmas.

Dan Kostopulos, Isis Theater manager, fulfilled wishes for Salt Lake City children. This article appeared in the *Salt Lake Tribune*, December 25, 1935.

As a penniless immigrant 14 years ago, Mr. Kostopulos knows what it means to be a youngster and not have the things that mean everything to such a child. So he has vowed that so far as he can prevent it, no child will meet Christmas without toys. Caring for 800 children would be a major job for a person of even robust income. To Mr. Kostopulos it is a real sacrifice which, he hastens to say, he is only too happy to make. He is an employee at the Broadway Theater. Surplus from his salary he conserves to bring this Christmas joy. He owns no car, uses no tobacco nor intoxicants and refrains from extravagant pleasures. As a result, he builds this sub for Santa fund.

—*Deseret News*
December 11, 1934

In the 1960s, Dan Kostopulos with his wife, Helene Pappas Kostopulos, established Camp Kostopulos in Emigration Canyon near Salt Lake City. Today the facility, known as Kostopulos Dream Foundation/Camp Kostopulos, is a year-round center that provides services for persons with all types of disabilities.

1918: The Minos Chapter of the Pan Cretan Association of America (PAA) was started in Salt Lake City. Beginning with 35 members, the chapter had more than 400 members from Utah, Nevada, and Wyoming by the end of 1918. Sam Kounalis, one of the founding fathers of Minos, first introduced the idea of a national association. The idea quickly gained momentum and, when the first PAA convention was held in Chicago in 1929, Kounalis was elected general secretary. Over the years, the chapter has continued to foster mutuality among Cretans, has provided financial support to Holy Trinity Cathedral and Prophet Elias Church, to the Hellenic Memorial Building, and to other charitable and educational causes.

Members of GAPA Olympus Lodge No. 60 are shown in a January 15, 1963, meeting. Peter Gamvroulas was president and Deno Kambouris vice president.

1925: The American Legion Hellenic Post No. 40 was initiated at a ceremony conducted by American Legion officials from the state office and from Post No. 2. Officers were: Peter S. Marthakis, commander; William Fotes, vice commander; Michael Katsanevas, treasurer; Jim Zafires; James C. Skedros, chaplain; and Jim Latsis, sergeant at arms.

1926: The Society of Athansios Diakos was established in Bingham Canyon by 26 men who banded together for the social, charitable, religious, and spiritual welfare of those who had emigrated to the U.S. from the central part of Greece. In addition, the organization has supported church, Greek language schools, charitable, cultural, and educational programs in Utah and in Greece. In the 1980s, Diakos opened its membership to women and to all Greeks. Today it has 175 members.

1927: The Panahaikos Society, Aghia Lavra, was established to be a patriotic, benevolent, and educational society of people from the state of Ahaioelidos, Greece. Its charitable program of assisting its members and their families in times of illness or death continued until February 1973, when it was dissolved.

1928: Olympus Lodge No. 60, Greek American Progressive Association (GAPA), was organized. Its main objectives were the retention of Greek culture, Greek Orthodoxy, and the Greek language, but they also placed importance on the development of good American citizenship. For many years the lodge was very active, sponsoring many socials and educational programs. In the 1930s, the lodge organized the GAPA Junior Band and the Demetra Club, a young women's group. The lodge was disbanded in 1982.

1928: Beehive Chapter No. 146, Order of the American Hellenic Educational Progressive Association (AHEPA) was organized. Nationally, the group was organized in 1922, as a way to counter anti-Greek discrimination and prejudices. English was the official language of the group and one of its principal objectives was to develop good American citizenship among Greek immigrants. When it was first organized the Salt Lake chapter sponsored the Sons of Pericles, the Maids of Athens, and the AHEPA Junior Band. The group continues its philanthropic activities today.

1929: Sappho Lodge No. 21, the women's auxiliary to GAPA, was organized to work for the development and preservation of the Greek language and to strengthen the religious beliefs of its members in accordance with the teachings of the Greek Orthodox Church. It was particularly active from 1956 to 1978, when it was disbanded.

1938: The Daughters of Minos was organized as an auxiliary to the Minos Chapter and is still active in preserving Cretan and Hellenic ideals and customs and in doing charitable work. In 2002, the PAA presented the Daughters with an award recognizing it for the largest increase in membership and for maintaining a base of 150 members. For the past 24 years, the group has supported the annual Greek Festival by preparing approximately 30,000 *dolmathes* for the event.

1938: A small number of Arcadian men met and organized an Arcadian Brotherhood Chapter which they named Theodoros Kolokotronis. In 1947, the chapter became Lodge No. 90 of the Pan Arcadian Federation of America. A women's auxiliary, Arcadia, was founded in 1942. Today, the Salt Lake chapter includes men and women and continues to raise funds for educational, religious, and charitable purposes.

1939: Greek women in Bingham Canyon organized the Ariadne Society. Its activities included promoting programs on Greek Independence Day and staging numerous *horosperithes* (evening socials), for the mining town's Greeks, through the

Daughters of Minos photographed during the 1970s, has maintained a large, active membership.

1950s. By the 1960s, Kennecott Copper Corporation was buying all the land and by 1970, Bingham Canyon was only a memory.

1939: Chari Chapter No. 79 of the Daughters of Penelope, the women's auxiliary to AHEPA, was organized with 20 charter members. The organization's name is derived from the character in Greek mythology, Penelope, who was the faithful wife of Odysseus and embodied all of the virtues of womanhood. It has contributed to such projects as the Hellenic Memorial Building, Aid to the Blind in Greece, and to numerous national and local charities.

1943: The Ladies Auxiliary of the Panahaikos Society, Mega Spilaion, was started and offered membership to those from, or related to someone, from the Greek states of Ahaia and Ilia, in the northwestern part of the Peloponnesus. In addition to mutual aid, their purpose was to encourage women of Greek nationality to become U.S. citizens and to inculcate American ideals in women of Greek nationality. The organization has continued through the years, and today its 38 members include daughters, daughters-in-law, and granddaughters of the first members. In an unusual turnabout in 2003, auxiliary members voted to allow men whose background was from these areas in Greece to become members since the men's organization had been disbanded.

Youth Groups

Youth groups appeared in the 1950s, when a Greek Orthodox Youth of America (GOYA) chapter was organized, with Senior, Junior, and Lamb groups. In 1951, the Salt Lake Cretan Juniors became a chapter of the national organization. Youth dance groups, beginning with Dionysus in 1970, evolved from these organizations and also continue to have age-group troupes, which perform at the Greek Festivals.

Fraternal Organizations

Pan Hellenic Union, Salt Lake City	*1908–1920*
Pan Hellenic Union, Bingham Canyon	*1908–1920*
Pan Hellenic Union, Scofield	*1908–1920*
Pan Hellenic Union, Castle Gate	*1912–1920*
Vyzas Society—Megara	*1915–1980*
Pan Cretan Association of	
America, Minos Chapter	*1918–*
Daughters of Minos	*1939–*
Cretan Juniors	*1950–1980*
Minotavros Group	*1980–*
Elpis Society (women)	*1920–1930*
Hellenic Post No. 40, American Legion	*1925–1940*
Society of Athanasios Diakos	*1926–*

Members of Sappho Lodge - GAPA in this 1950s photo, include standing in front Georgia Teseros, Mrs. Gus Kaddas, Angeline Marganis, Tasia Vasilacopoulos, District Governor George Zeese, Olympia Demiris, Stamatina Latsomanis, Helen Rizos, Demetra Kambouris, Mrs. Kargas. In second row Kaliopie Ligdas, Pipina Rovolis, Bessie Souvall, Olga Kalantzes, Kome Souvall, Emily Zeese, Angeline Deneris, Popie Kosta, Angeline Skedros, Rozalia Zaharias, Angeline Goudi. In third row Mary Liapis, Mrs. Xenakis, Sophie Polychronis, Mary Jackson, Angeline Kanell, Mrs. Kitchopoulos, Helen Bowden. In top row Fr. Antonios Kalogeropoulos, Mrs. Pappas, Mrs. Lendaris, Maria Halles, Mary Katsanevas, Helen Jouflas, and Irene Rondas.

Panahaikos Society Agia Lavra	*1927–1973*
Ladies Group Mega Spilaion	*1943*
American Educational Hellenic	
Progressive Association, AHEPA	
Beehive Chapter No. 146, Salt Lake City	*1928–*
Bonneville Chapter No. 324, Salt Lake City	*1935–1960*
Bingham Canyon Chapter No. 183	*1929–1950*
Ogden, Utah Chapter No. 184	*1929–*
Daughters of Penelope	*1939–*
Maids of Athens	*1937–*
Sons of Pericles	*1937–*
Greek American Progressive Association, GAPA	
Olympus Lodge No. 60	*1924–1982*
Sappho Lodge (women's auxiliary)	*1929–1978*
Demetra Young Women's Group	*1930–1950*
Bachelors 47 Club (Athletic)	*1931–1940*
Hellenic Athletic Group	*1932–1940*
Arcadian Society	
Kolokotronis Lodge	*1938–*
Ladies Society, Arcadia	*1942–*
Ariadne Ladies Society, Bingham Canyon	*1939–1965*
Hellenic Improvement Association, HIA	*1948–1955*
Hellenic Women's Club	*1970s–*
Young Orthodox Women	*1970s–*
Orthodox Men's Society	*1977–1981*
Hellenic Cultural Association	*1986–*
Hellenic Bar Association	*1990–*

Church Related:

Greek-Language school	*1915–*
Sunday Schools (Holy Trinity, Prophet Elias)	*1930s–*
Holy Trinity Choir	*1935–*
Hellenic Mothers' Club	*1935–1955*
Philoptochos Society	*1956–*
Prophet Elias Choir	*1969–*

Church Ministries 2005 — Leadership

Philoptochos Society of Holy Trinity	Margo Sotiriou, president
Philoptochos Society of Prophet Elias	Stephanie Chachas, president
Young Ladies Philoptochos, St. Cassaini	Ann Varanakis
Philoptochos Senior Citizens	Angelina Kontgis, Athena Davis, Anna Makris
Philoptochos Welfare	Dianne Johnson, Antoinette Sotiriou
Choir, Holy Trinity	George Miller
Choir, Prophet Elias	Paul Maritsas
Altar Boys	Fr. Elias Koucos
Y.A.L. (Young Adult League, 18–35 years of age)	Angela Parenti
Campus Ministry	Fr. Matthew Gilbert
Sunday School, Holy Trinity	Julie Fotes
Sunday School, Prophet Elias	Paul Karahalios
Dance Ministry Team	Fr. Matthew Gilbert
Young/Young Adult Ministry Team	Fr. Matthew Gilbert
Dionysus Dance (18 and older)	Georgiann Pino
Greek Orthodox Youth	
Sr. GOYA, coordinator/president grades 10–12	James Katsanevas
Jr. GOYA, coordinator/president grades 7–9	Manoli Liodakis
J.O.Y. and H.O.P.E., advisors, grades 4–6 and 1–3	Connie Cayias, Kristy Pappas, Niki Pazell
Lambs advisors, preschool	Stacy Kournianos, Connie Yengich
Athletic Director	Michael Daskalas
Greek School	Nitsa Tsoutsounakis
St. Sophia Orthodox School	Mary Ann Rees
Boy Scouts	Robert Nelson
Girl Scouts	Tia Athens
Brownies	Nicole Athens

Fraternal Organizations 2005

	Leadership
Daughters of Minos	Jill Kogianes
Minotavros	Sifi Sifantonakis
Minos Chapter	George Liodakis
Pan Arcadian Federation Chapter No. 90	George Anastasopoulos
Arcadian Ladies	Eleni Paloukos
AHEPA	Elias Pylidis
Daughters of Penelope	Aspasia Sakellariou
Sons of Pericles	John Pylidis
Society of Athanasios Diakos	Bill Kandas
Hellenic Cultural Association	Jim Kastanis
Hellenic Women	Madelyn Bowden
Panahaikos Society	Shelley Anderson

Board of Trustees Presidents, 1925–1940

Phillip Drandakis, 1925, 1926	Peter E. Athas, 1933, 1934
Peter C. Pitchios, 1927, 1928	John Kotsovos, 1935
Nicholas Melis, 1929	James Latsis, 1936
James Lambros, 1930	George Zeese, 1937, 1938
Ernest Chipian, 1931	John G. Condas, 1939
George Foundas, 1932	George Papanikolas, 1940

"It was hard (to raise funds to build the Hellenic Memorial Building.) It took a lot of hardship work. Unless you can go out there and beg, I'm telling you, it was pretty hard. But we managed it all right. We done pretty good job and we're proud that this new building is paid for and some for the new church, too. And so what more do you want? Nothing else."

—George Cayias, b. 1896
Greek Oral History Collection

Choir Approved; Youth Participate on Board

The church board approved establishment of a church choir in 1934. Such a plan had been presented years earlier but no action was taken. This time the idea took hold, and the first choir-enhanced Sunday services occurred the following year. Its first director was Constantine Milenopoulos who also served as chanter and teacher in the community until 1939.

Thirty years had passed since the Greek community was organized. During this time, immigrants from Greece were primarily responsible for the development and growth of the community. Looking ahead, the church's Board of Trustees seriously considered the role that the youth of the community would eventually play in the perpetuation of the Orthodox religion in the United States and in the administration of the Greek Orthodox Church-community of Salt Lake City and vicinity. To train the youth for this role, the board instituted a program wherein young people would attend all board meetings and participate in functions and activities as set forth by the community leaders. Selected to represent the younger generation in these activities were Louis P. Athas, George J. Condas, Gus Praggastis, and Ted J. Speros.

1935

To showcase its community spirit, the Greek church-community entered a float in the state's biggest celebration of the year, the Days of '47 Parade, held annually on July 24, in downtown Salt Lake City to commemorate the arrival of the Church of Jesus Christ of Latter-day Saints (Mormon) pioneers into the Salt Lake Valley in 1847. The float featured a scene of ancient Athens, with Harry G. Metos as Pericles addressing the Athenians. The float won first prize among all entries, a recognition that brought great honor to the Greeks of Utah.

May 10, 1936: Archbishop Athenagoras, the head of the Greek Orthodox Church in North and South America, visited Salt Lake City. *The Salt Lake Tribune* reported the event as follows:

Greek Orthodox Church Head Visits in Salt Lake
Archbishop Athenagoras Officiates at Mass; Sees Rebirth of Religious Interest; 250 Receive Communion Rites

The Most Rev. Archbishop Athenagoras, head of the Greek Orthodox Church of North and South America, officiated at mass Sunday morning in the local church, opening his three-day visitation to the Salt Lake City Greek Community.

Following the mass, nearly 250 faithful received communion from his grace.

The prelate addressed the communicants on the benefits of faithful religious service, urging them to accept and guard the tenets of the church.

Rebirth of Interest

A wide rebirth of religious interest in America at the present time was seen by Archbishop Athenagoras.

"Depression years have taught us that we must have a sustaining belief if we would be happy," his grace said. "In all fields we feel this new belief, this leaning toward religion. Science is religious now. Scientific researches are religious researches."

From the new "brotherhood of churches" movement there will come great strengthening of religious and greater understanding, he declared.

"Ultimately this movement will lead to unification of churches, to a universal church. But not for the moment," the Archbishop said. "Right now we must strive to remove petty differences."

Seek Same Things

Since all churches are seeking the same thing, differing only in their methods, removal of such misunderstandings will greatly strengthen our religious life, Archbishop Athenagoras said.

The official was guest of the local church at a luncheon in the afternoon and addressed ladies of the church at a Mother's Day

Archbishop Athenagoras, 1936.

*service in the church parlors in the evening. Monday he will
visit with Governor Henry H. Blood, Mayor E. G. Erwin and
other officials.*

*He was met in Pocatello, Idaho, Saturday by P. S. Marthakis
and C. [Chris] E. Athas of Salt Lake City and motored with
them to the city. They were accompanied by the Rev. Archdeacon
Nicodemos, assistant secretary of the headquarters of the
church, and the Rev. Stamatio of the Church of the Assumption
at Pocatello.*

*When he returns to his headquarters at Long Island, N.Y.,
he will have visited 250 cities in the United States.*

—*Salt Lake Tribune*
May 10, 1936

A bevy of Greek beauties of the 1930s included Zeffie Pappas, standing left, Helen Fotis, Koula Pikoulas, Helen Paulos, Wilma Fotis, Stella Pappas; Vasiliki Pikoulas, front left, Maria Cairo and Harriet Fotis.

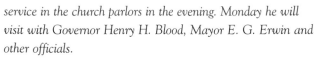

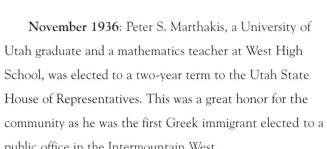

Peter S. Marthakis played football for the University of Utah in 1916.

November 1936: Peter S. Marthakis, a University of Utah graduate and a mathematics teacher at West High School, was elected to a two-year term to the Utah State House of Representatives. This was a great honor for the community as he was the first Greek immigrant elected to a public office in the Intermountain West.

Jimmy Londos, "The Golden Greek," was in Salt Lake to visit relatives and friends and was ready to defend his title as the world's professional wrestling champion.

—*Deseret News*
September 4, 1937

During 1936 and 1938, the church leadership devoted its attention to streamlining bylaws that governed the church-community, including changing the community's name. Under the original articles of incorporation, drawn in 1905, the organization's name was "The Greek Community of Utah." This was appropriate at the time because the only Greek Orthodox Church in Utah was in Salt Lake City. That changed in 1916, with the organization of the Greek Orthodox community in Price. Therefore, in 1936, the name of the Salt Lake City church-community was changed to the "Hellenic Orthodox Church Holy Trinity." In 1938, the name was changed again, this time to "The Greek Community of Utah." Ten months later, it became the "Greek Orthodox Church Holy Trinity of Salt Lake City, Utah." In 2005, the official name is "The Greek Orthodox Church of Greater Salt Lake."

Under article four of the articles of incorporation, the church recognized as its ecclesiastical spiritual head the Ecumenical Patriarchate of Constantinople. It also recognized the Archdiocese of North and South America as the spiritual representative of the Ecumenical Patriarchate. In addition, it specifically reserved to the community members all of the properties and assets of the organization.

1939

The beauty of the Holy Trinity Church and the image of the Salt Lake City Greek community were both enhanced in 1939.

The importance of the Holy Trinity Church choir was fully recognized when a qualified director, H. Fredrick Davis, was hired. Even though he did not know the Greek language,

A 1939 party for the Sons of Pericles and the Maids of Athens attracted this large group.

the choir blossomed under his leadership, rapidly becoming one of the finest religious vocal groups of the city and of the Greek Orthodox Churches in the United States.

The services of a professional iconographer were procured to decorate the interior walls of the Holy Trinity Church with Byzantine icons for the first time. Efstathios A. Nikos of Kansas City, Missouri, undertook the four-year project.

The Salt Lake Greek Orthodox Church was officially represented at the Clergy-Laity Congress of the Greek Orthodox in San Francisco.

Athletic Activities Today the Salt Lake Greek community's youth participate in numerous sports programs—mostly basketball. But that wasn't always the case. Participating in organized athletics during the formative years of the community was not a priority for the Greeks because they were busy with other activities.

A basketball team comprised of second-generation Greeks born in America was organized in 1930 and played under the banner of AHEPA Junior Basketball. Its roster consisted of Andrew Takis, Napoleon C. Dokos, William G. Dokos, James G. Dokos, Steve Pantelakis, Basil Delis, and Chris G. Dokos.

Many second generation Greek Americans attended Salt Lake City's West High School—enough to form a sizeable Hellenic Club, shown here in 1940 with Peter S. Marthakis, mathematics teacher and club advisor.

In 1931, the Bachelors 47 Club was organized to promote fellowship and sport participation among men in the community. Under its bylaws, one had to be between the ages of 17 and 30 and be unmarried to become a member, hence the "47."

Members of the two branches of the Dokos family living in Salt Lake loved playing baseball. One roster from the mid-1930s lists seven players named Dokos: George, James (Doc), and Napoleon of one branch of the family and Andy, Chris, Bill, and Jim from the other family. Also on the team were Jack Argentos, Andy Takis, Peter J. Pitchess, Marty Vandini, Steve Pantelakis, Pete Love, and George Zolintakis.

Leagues and Tournaments

Local Greek basketball and baseball teams were fielded in the mid-1930s and played under the name of the Hellenics. These rosters included Louis P. Athas, Nicholas L. Strike, George Morris, George Marinakis, Peter Pitchess, (an all-state basketball player from Bingham High School), Sam Velis, Cosmo Cairo, Ted Kisciras, and George Floor. Playing for an AHEPA-sponsored team during this period were: John E. Papanikolas, Nick E. Papanikolas, Ernest Paulos, Nick Theos, and William P. Athas. In 1937, a Sons of Pericles team from Bingham won the league championship following an 18 to 11 victory over the Sons of Pericles Salt Lake team. Players from both teams were invited to participate in the Sons of Pericles National Tournament in Pittsburgh. Coached by Andrew Takis, the Utah entry was made up of John Mannos, Mike Leventis, John Chipian, Pete Dimas, and George Anagnostakis. In 1939, the Salt Lake Sons of Pericles team consisted of Leo and Ernest Kanell, Nick and George Theos, Chris Tsouras, Cosmo Cairo, Tike and Chris Luras, and Andrew G. Dokos.

Interest in participating in organized athletics during World War II waned as the Greek community became preoccupied by more pressing issues. But soon after the war, interest in sports was rekindled and the Greek community entered the Hellenics in the Salt Lake area Young Men's Christian Association (YMCA) Church League. This team included Jimmy Brown, Nick Vidalakis, and George C. Furgis.

Her father and uncle Steve arranged for her and her two sisters, Katherine and Mary to come to U.S. They stayed on Ellis Island until someone picked them up and put them on a train for Salt Lake.

"...and a lady was waiting for us every stop we made, to get off, to change trains. Like in Chicago...

"We were just huddled together like three little lambs. What an experience. I guess because we were too small and didn't think or fear of what would happen to us. We got along fine."

—May Gooras, b. 1912
Greek Oral History Collection

The AHEPA basketball team brought trophies home in 1949. Team members included Nick Psarras, left, John Calevas, Cosmo Cairo, Louis P. Athas, George Dimas, Andy Takis, George Furgis, John Sefakis, Jimmy Brown, Nick Theos, Nick Vidalakis, and Basil Anton.

"Well, I'll be honest with you. In the first years I come here in 1909 (and) up to 1919, for 10 years, all the nationalities, they were suffering here in Utah from the citizens of Utah. Because they think we didn't know anything, because we come from some strange country. Especially the Scandinavians, they hated us. But after 1920 and later, the marriages come between both sides."

—*Paul Borovilos*
Greek Oral History Collection

In 1947, the Hellenic softball team recorded a 24–2 won-lost record in the Inter-Church League of Salt Lake City. It was made up of Jimmy Arkoudas, George Theos, Nick Comas, John J. Ypsilantis, George Nicolatus, Jerry Kladis, Cosmo Cairo, Chris Luras, and John Kumarelas.

The Rocky Mountain Hellenic Basketball Tournament was unveiled in Denver in 1948. The Salt Lake team swept to the championship due to the play of Bill Anton, Louis Athas, Jimmy Brown, John Calevas, Cosmo Cairo, George Dimas, George Furgis, Nick Psarras, John Sefakis, Nick Theos, Nick Vidalakis, and coach Andy Takis.

Salt Lake City played host to the 1952 Rocky Mountain Hellenic Basketball Tournament in the new Hellenic Memorial Building. Thirteen teams from all parts of the United States participated in a tournament that was won by Chicago after defeating a team from Magna in the finals. The Magna team consisted of Jim Colovos, Arthur Flangas, Gus Klekas, Mike Klekas, Bill Klekas, Bill Patsuris, John Prokopis, and Bill Prokopis.

To celebrate its 50th anniversary, the Salt Lake Greek community teamed with the local chapter of the Greek Orthodox Youth of America (GOYA) to host the 1955 Rocky Mountain Hellenic Basketball Tournament, which attracted 12 teams. The Salt Lake All-Stars, Salt Lake GOYA, and Magna represented the local community.

Members of the Salt Lake All-Stars team were: Sam Babalis, Bob Babalis, Jim Babalis, Pete Jouflas, George L. Strike, Andy Pete Souvall, and Peter Vrontikis. The Salt Lake GOYA team consisted of Jimmy Brown, Pete Comas, George Furgis, Nick Jouflas, Nick Loulias, Mike Loulias, Nick Sefakis, John Sefakis, Andy Takis, and Gus Teseros. The Salt Lake Hellenics' roster had George Argentos, Jim Bapis, Chris Ballamis, Gus Jackson, Tom C. Korologos, Dean Kastanis, George Poulos, Ernest Psarras, Leo Sotiriou, Tommie Sotiriou, John Xanthos, and Nick Psarras.

Women's Teams

The Greek Orthodox community was among the first to form female teams to participate in organized inter-church recreational programs after World War II. When the Young Women's Christian Association (YWCA) Girls Inter-Church Softball League was organized in 1949, the Greek community was well represented. On the Hellenic Improvement Association (HIA) team were Argie Adondakis, Eugenia Batestas, Teddy Arnold, Martha Castles, Barbara Cozakos, Lucille Cozakos, Helen Kladis, Kay Kladis, Charlene Kouris, Mary Marganis, Emily Marganis, Mary Maragakis, Helen Rondas, Mary Shupit, Margo Sotiriou, and Fannie Zaharias.

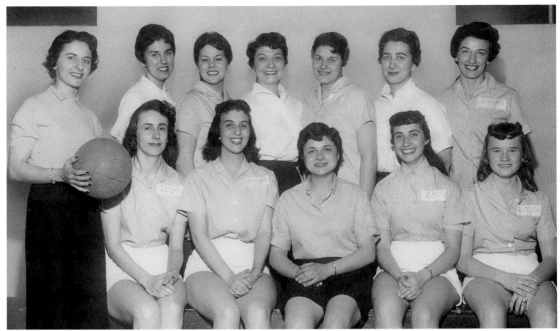

Members of a women's basketball team in the late 1940s–early 1950s were Mary Maragakis, standing left, Helen Anagnostakis, Elaine Polychronis, Elsie Gaviotis, Sophie Makris, Elaine Batestas, Emily Marganis; Wilma Dimas, seated left, Helen Kouris, Leah Pappas, Lucille Cozakos, and Becky Takis.

Since that time, men's and women's softball and basketball programs have been important parts of the recreational activities involving the youth of the community. The numerous trophies on display at the Hellenic Memorial Building and at Prophet Elias Church are impressive reminders of the success of these programs and serve as tributes to their coaches and volunteers.

Greek women worked with the American Red Cross in Salt Lake City in 1943–1945, doing hand-stitching. Seated at back are Mrs. Nick Anton, left, Helen Rizos, Mrs. Gus Kaddas, Angeline Skedros, Mrs. Peter Zolintakis. Among those seated in front are Anna Mouskondis, left, Christina Strike, fourth from left, Katherine Zerefos, and Katherine Kitchopoulos.

Chapter 4

The War Years Through 1959

In October 1940, the invasion of Greece by Italy and the German attack there, in April 1941, vividly brought the war in Europe close to the Greek community. In 1941, the Greek War Relief Association was organized nationally, and Peter S. Marthakis was appointed Utah director of this program. Peter E. Athas became Salt Lake County director. A separate church committee was appointed to solicit contributions from its members. Between 1941 and 1942 this group collected more than $10,000 for the Greek War Relief Fund. The statewide drive contributed additional thousands of dollars. The sacrifices experienced during this period in the Salt Lake Greek community inspired both mother country Greek and Greek-American fervor for volunteerism and church-community devotion to betterment.

Fr. Antonios Kalogeropoulos officiated at the baptism of Elaine C. Korologos in Holy Trinity Church in 1948. Ernest G. Mantes was the godfather.

The Japanese attack on Pearl Harbor on December 7, 1941 engulfed the country in World War II and the youth of the Greek community answered the call to arms.

The war outcome was on the minds of everyone as its impact had reached into nearly all the homes of the community. Some 450 members of the community were in the armed forces. Gold Star banners, signifying a family member was serving in the U.S. Armed Forces, hung with pride in the windows of Greek homes. Many families had members who were killed or wounded in action.

The following parish members made the supreme sacrifice in World War II

Capt. William P. Athas
Lt. James A. Batestas
Cpl. Nicholas R. Bowden
Pfc. George G. Colovos
Pfc. Theodore C. Dimas
Lt. Peter N. Dontas
Pfc. Leo G. Kanell

Sgt. Bill P. Karabatsos
Pfc. George Kastanis
Lt. George L. Latches
Lt. John G. Papadopoulos (Pappas)
Lt. Sam J. Sdrales
Lt. Robert G. Stamos

Captain Steve N. Floor, died later as a result of his war wounds.

The church board decided to set aside the Sunday of Orthodoxy for memorial services honoring the dead of World War II. This was to be an annual observance. In addition, a committee was appointed to assist returning veterans to obtain jobs and assimilate, once again, into the community so they could return to "a normal life" as soon as possible.

Community Social Center For many years,

acquiring or building a community social center had been the subject of numerous discussions. In fact, the Greek immigrants of 1908 had talked about such a center. In 1943, the idea was still in the discussion stage.

Up to this time most social affairs staged by the community or by the various fraternal organizations were held in the lower level hall of Holy Trinity Church. As the

Memorial services for Captain William P. Athas were held at Holy Trinity Church, 1952. His parents, Peter and Anna Athas, are shown at left.

Steve J. Poulos, a World War II veteran, was seriously wounded in Normandy, June 1944.

community grew, these facilities became inadequate for events of any appreciable size.

At the general assembly of 1943, a proposal to build a community center was presented and a committee was formed and charged to do a feasibility study. Soon thereafter, the church board purchased two home sites north of Holy Trinity Church for $10,000. Board members reasoned that if a recreational center were to be built, it should be adjacent to the church.

A committee was appointed to oversee construction of the proposed community center at a special meeting of the general assembly on October 24. Its duties were to buy the property adjacent to the Holy Trinity Church, collect contributions for construction of the center, contract the building of the center, and conduct fund-raising campaigns in the community. Committee members were George Zeese, Peter E. Athas, Peter S. Marthakis, Sam Kounalis, Gust C. Captain, Gus Anton, and George Cayias.

The building committee collected more than $13,500, of which $10,500 was used to purchase the property north of Holy Trinity. The remaining amount was placed in the building fund.

Post World War II

An increasing number of younger community members actively participated in various church functions from 1946–1949, and this enthusiasm was a major factor in bringing about the construction of the proposed social center.

The younger group, together with many older members of the church, believed it was time for the church to obtain the services of an additional clergyman. Church leaders, cognizant of the growing number of American-born members, said it was imperative that the new clergyman be well versed in English and Greek and be a native-born American.

The emphasis on keeping the younger Greeks from drifting away from the church was further noted by the fact that in 1947 the bylaws of the community were being printed in Greek and English.

The Hellenic Improvement Association (HIA) was organized in 1947–1948 by community youth. Founders were Chris S. Metos, John Delis, Chris Demiris, John Maragakis, Kay Dimas, Fannie Zaharias, Mary Kumarelas, John L. Strike, and Constantine J. Skedros, who wrote the constitution of the newly formed group. For the next several years, most HIA activities were devoted to church and community affairs. It actively participated in raising funds for the oft-mentioned social/recreation center, and for several years it published a newspaper—the *Agia Trias News*.

Through the efforts of the HIA, similar groups were formed in Price, Pocatello, and Denver. The Rocky Mountain area groups interacted with youth groups from Oakland and San Francisco. These associations forged the way for the establishment of the Greek Orthodox Youth of America (GOYA) that the Greek Archdiocese organized in the mid-1950s. Ultimately, the HIA chapter became part of GOYA.

Greek Officials Elected

In 1946, Salt Lake City attorney William Cayias, Jr., (D) was elected to a two-year term in the Utah State House of Representatives. That same year Peter S. Marthakis (D), a former member of the Utah State House of Representatives, was elected to a four-year term to the Utah State Senate.

In 1947, even though World War II ended in victory for the democracies of the world, the people of war-ravaged Greece

George Cayias, on stand left, John E. Papanikolas and his mother Georgia Papanikolas at microphone, participated in 1949 ground breaking ceremony for Hellenic Memorial Building

continued to suffer from the calamities and deprivations resulting from wars. In addition to the famine, death, destruction, and misery brought about by the German occupation, the country was embroiled in a civil war. U.S. aid to Greece in 1947 included that given by the Church of Jesus Christ of Latter-day Saints (LDS, Mormon), based in Salt Lake City. The LDS Church contributed 60,000 pounds of wheat to Greece.

In 1948, Greeks residing in the West Jordan area of Salt Lake Valley moved toward construction of a Greek school and recreation center to serve the needs of those living in Midvale, West Jordan, and Bingham. George Adondakis

donated the land for a building. The church's executive committee appointed Nick Kouris, Jim Varanakis, and Pete Loulias to assist Adondakis with the building effort.

1949–1950 Memorial Building

During 1949 and 1950, the church made progress toward building a community social center to be known as the Hellenic Memorial Building, in honor of those who had served in the armed forces. The newly elected Board of Trustees included four members from the younger generation: John Chipian, Peter Dimas, Chris Metos, and Constantine J. Skedros.

The church had collected $42,000 for the center by the time construction started. Not wishing to negotiate a bank loan to complete the project, the board called a general assembly where it was decided to transfer $30,000 from the church treasury to the building treasury to complete the work. Total cost of the Memorial Building was approximately $125,000.

Groundbreaking took place September 4, 1949, and was attended by many parish members and by civic dignitaries. During this event, some major contributions to the project were made by Georgia Papanikolas, $1,600; the Mothers Club, $2,500; and Mrs. Harry Miles, $2,000.

On October 30, bidding for name recognition on the four cornerstones of the new building resulted in additional contributions from Mrs. George Zeese, $1,500; Mrs. Gregory Soter, $1,400; Mrs. Angeline Kanell, $1,000; and George Cayias, $500.

Nick Galanis and Andy Luras were co-chairs of the Greek community's first carnival, to be distinguished from the current annual Greek Festival, in May 1950. It was the largest three-day community social event ever staged by the Greek community and raised $10,000 for the building.

The Alvin Youngberg firm drafted architectural plans and construction began on September 13, 1949. The church board, which was acting as a general building committee, appointed Sam Soter to deal with subcontractors. Peter S. Marthakis and John E. Papanikolas also assisted in supervising construction. On October 21, 1950, the Hellenic Memorial Building was officially opened to the Greek community.

Highlights of the Period

January 1950: Nicholas G. Cozakos was named choir director at Holy Trinity Church, succeeding Frederick Davis. Cozakos had been with the choir nearly a decade and had coordinated services for Davis. Cozakos served as choir director at Holy Trinity Church until 1968. Other choir directors at Holy Trinity were Stella Pantelakis, Paul Maritsas, Jim Tsoufakis, Basil Chelemes, and current director George Miller. Maritsas has served as choir director at Prophet Elias Church since 1969.

May 1950: the general assembly authorized the board to purchase the property north of the Hellenic Memorial Building for a sum not to exceed $9,000.

1951–1955

January 1951: The general assembly increased annual dues for church membership to $12. The Clergy-Laity Congress of 1950 increased dues payable to the Archdiocese to $10 per family.

March 24, 1951: The 130th anniversary of Greek independence was celebrated with a banquet in the new Hellenic Memorial Building. Chris S. Metos was chairman and John B. Sergakis was toastmaster. Guest speakers were Dr. L.R. McKay, professor of Modern Languages, University of

The Hellenic Memorial Building was the location for this 1952 banquet celebrating Greek Independence Day.

Exuberant men dance at an early 1950s celebration. From left, Chris T. Korologos, Ernest G. Mantes, Triantafilos Gouvisis, Bill Manes, Pete Aleferis, and John Thiros.

Women formed their own lines for more restrained dancing. From left, Irene Korologos, Virginia Politz, Angela Psarras and her mother, Maxine.

Utah; Rev. George Weber, pastor of First Congregational Church, and Constantine J. Skedros representing the Salt Lake Greek community.

1952: Construction of the West Jordan Greek School and Social Building was completed.

July 1952: Holy Trinity Choir hosted the convention of the Western States Choir Federation of the Greek Orthodox Church. Among the highlights was a concert in the Assembly Hall on Salt Lake City's Temple Square. It featured authentic Byzantine hymns and a nationwide radio broadcast of 150 voices singing the liturgy in the Hellenic Memorial Building. Bishop Athenogoras officiated at the service during the broadcast.

May 1953: The initial conference of the Fourth Diocese of the Greek Orthodox Youth of America and the Philoptochos Society was held in Salt Lake City. Bishop Athenagoras and delegates from GOYA chapters of the 11 Western states attended.

March 1954: Holy Trinity Choir attained international prominence when it performed the Greek National Anthem in the Salt Lake Mormon Tabernacle during a concert of the Utah Symphony Orchestra. This performance was rebroadcast in Athens, Greece, via the Voice of America.

1954: After serving the parish for nearly 10 years, Fr. Antonios Kalogeropoulos asked for a transfer to a smaller parish. Fr. George Pulos was assigned to succeed him. He served in Salt Lake until the spring of 1955 when Fr. George Mestakides, who served for a very short time, succeeded him. In May 1955, Fr. Steven A. Katsaris was assigned to Holy Trinity Church. During the seven years he served, Fr. Katsaris helped prepare a new curriculum for the Sunday school and was very active with youth programs. He also was very prominent in the non-Greek community of Salt Lake City.

May 1, 1955: A bronze statue of Lycurgus, King and Law Giver of Ancient Sparta was unveiled at the Utah State Capitol. It was created by Avard Fairbanks, internationally recognized Utah sculptor, and was commissioned by the Phalanx of the Knights of Thermopylae. Leroy Robertson, of the University of Utah music department, wrote a composition commemorating the Battle of Thermopylae for this event. The statue of Lycurgus was placed in the main square of Sparta, Greece, on July 1, 1955. Parishioners Chris and Alice Athas were the prime movers of these events.

1955: The golden anniversary of the founding of the Greek Orthodox Church in Utah was commemorated in various ways under co-chairs William G. Dokos and Chris Demiris. A 50th anniversary book in Greek and English was produced under the leadership of Constantine J. Skedros, John N. Maragakis, William D. Cocorinis, and James C. Dokos. Dokos summarized notes from minutes of major meetings held from 1905 to 1955, which were written in Greek. Skedros, assisted by Maragakis, wrote the English section while Cocorinis wrote the Greek section.

Another highlight of the 50th anniversary was a banquet in the Memorial Building on October 30, 1955. Guest speakers were Bishop Demetrios, Bishop of the Western States Diocese of the Greek Orthodox Church; Utah Governor J. Bracken Lee; Dr. A. Ray Olpin, president of the University of Utah; and Ted J. Speros, president of the Greek community. Honored at this banquet were 24 of the living pioneers who were in Salt Lake City in 1905 when the Greek community was organized. Several others did not attend.

Greek 1905 Pioneers Honored

William Andrews	Stelios Faraos
Peter E. Athas	George Foundas
James Batestas	John Kerikas
George Castles	Peter S. Marthakis
William Cayias	Nick Melis
George Cozakos	Christ Pappasotiriou
Jim Demiris	Tom Praggastis
Gus Delis	John Speros
Andrew Dokos	Steve Stavropoulos
George Dokos	George N. Strike
George Floor	James Velis
Nick Floor	Peter Xenakis

"See, the old-timers, some of them still live in the Julian Calendar. Some don't. Well, we had that misunderstanding in a lot of communities in the United States. But Salt Lake, here, even if we believe different, we didn't divide. We stick together."

—*Paul Borovilos*
Greek Oral History Collection

The March 2005 membership tea for the Philoptochos Society attracted a crowd. Nola Slager, president at the time, is seated third from the left.

Philoptochos Society One of the most important church-affiliated organizations came into existence during 1955–56 when the Hellenic Mothers' Club became a chapter of the National Philoptochos Society. Fr. Harry Gavalas and his Presbytera (wife) were honored by a group of women in the community in 1935, and he saw the need for a formally organized group. Under his initiative, the Mothers' Club was formed and became an auxiliary of the church. The first president was Emily Zeese. Dues were 10 cents per month; widows paid five cents and if they couldn't afford that, they could join anyway.

In its early years, members of the Mothers' Club mended clothes for the poor, administered to the sick and needy, helped baptize children, and participated in all church activities. Their efforts also supported the Greek War Relief, the local Red Cross, United Service Organization (USO) snack bars, and they represented Greece at the World Bazaar of the Young Women's Christian Association (YWCA).

After becoming the Philoptochos Society, the group continued to help people in need and its efforts expanded to meet the changing times. Philoptochos today is a prime source of hospitality for community projects and receptions. It sponsors senior citizen events, and donates funds and personnel to many worthy causes, including the Metropolis of Denver and national programs.

Church Reforms Instituted In January 1956, Fr. Katsaris recommended sweeping reforms regarding church improvements and a religious education program for the youth. He noted that Salt Lake City was a center of learning and culture and a hub of religious, educational, and business activities of the Intermountain West. This provided a "a unique opportunity for the Greek Orthodox Church of Salt Lake City to become the focal point and showplace of Orthodoxy in this vast area," he wrote.

Fr. Katsaris pointed out that a growing awareness of Orthodox Christianity had resulted in his speaking to various groups and in visits by non-orthodox groups to Holy Trinity Church. "By and large, our non-orthodox friends judge us by our external appearances, our church structure, its interior decorations, our deportment during worship, etc. We would do well, therefore, if we undertook to make our church building and community center, our worship services, etc., real show places of traditional Orthodoxy."

He recommended 22 church improvements, including installation of a chanter's stand and a bishop's throne, refinishing of the iconostasion, general interior painting and decoration and exterior cleaning and painting of the church building, acquisition of an appropriate baptismal font, and installation of a bulletin board for the church grounds.

Fr. Katsaris pointed out the inadequacy of the Sunday school program because of lack of suitable teaching space and equipment, over-crowded classes, and outside interferences interrupting the teaching process. He recommended that each class should consist of no more than 10–15 students, suggested additional Sunday school rooms be provided on the lower level of the church, that collapsible partitions be

Bishop Demetrios of the Los Angeles Diocese with the Holy Trinity Church Board of Trustees in 1958. Fr. Steven A. Katsaris, left, Peter Tasoulis, Chris Georgelas, James Cozakos, Ted Jouflas, John Karpakis, Peter Vrontikis, Bishop Demetrios, William Cocorinis (President), Peter Alex, Mike Varanakis, James Cononelos, John Gacanis, Pete Gustas, John L. Strike, George Dokos, Fr. James Adams, and Nick Loucas.

Clergy-Laity Conference, Salt Lake City, July 1958. Fr. Steven A. Katsaris, standing left, Bishop Demetrios, Bishop Ezekiel, Bishop Fifinis, sixth from left, and Fr. James Adams; Bishop Germanos, seated left, and President David O. McKay of the Church of Jesus Christ of Latter-day Saints.

installed in the Memorial Building classrooms, and that a wing be added to the Memorial Building, designed in such a way so that during the week it could be converted to space for activities of church and community organizations.

He proposed a "Dollar-a-Week Church Improvement Club" and a "Dollar-a-Sunday Religious Education Club" to help fund the recommendations, including a future church nursery school and a parochial school.

His recommendations were unanimously adopted at the first meeting of the Holy Trinity Church Board of Trustees in 1956. Most of his recommendations were implemented by 1958.

1957–1958

February 1957: John E. Papanikolas was named general chairman for the 14th Biennial Clergy-Laity Congress of the Greek Orthodox Archdiocese of North and South America scheduled for June 1958. Constantine J. Skedros and Gust J. Anton were named co-chairs and Sam W. Souvall treasurer.

In anticipation of the congress, improvements were made to the interior of Holy Trinity Church, including the addition of stained-glass windows and the installation of an electric organ. The Louis N. Strike family was a major donor for many of these improvements. Iconographer Alexander Sideris, New York City, was hired to paint a new Platetera, Pantokrator, and the Four Evangelists. James G. Pappas made a major donation in memory of his parents, Constantine and Evgenia Papadopoulos (Pappas) for this purpose.

In 1958, Ernest G. Mantes (D) was appointed to the Utah State Senate to finish the term of a state senator who had died. Mantes represented Tooele and Juab counties from 1958 to 1972. Highly regarded among his peers and constituents, he was known in the senate as a fiscal conservative.

Clergy-Laity Congress

A high point for the community in 1958 was the staging of the Clergy-Laity Congress June 29–July 5. Eighteen committees comprised of more than 200 members helped stage the event. Archbishop Michael, the spiritual leader of the Greek Orthodox Church of North and South America, presided. Unfortunately, during the Congress the Archbishop became ill and was hospitalized. He died shortly after his return to New York.

The Congress attracted representatives from 101 parishes, 75 clergy, 300 lay delegates, the Archdiocese staff from New York City and five bishops. A grand banquet drew more than 850 attendees. Proceeds from the Congress were used to purchase property north of the Memorial Building in 1959.

The *Salt Lake Tribune* reported the event:

Welcome, Churchmen

Salt Lake City and Utah are proud to play host this week to the Biennial Ecclesiastical Congress of the Greek Orthodox Church of North and South America.

Although there is a substantial Greek community in Utah, and many of its leaders are very active in Greek Orthodox Church affairs, this is the first time the biennial congress has been held in the state. It is a tribute to Utah and to its citizens of Greek ancestry that this church, which has more than a million members in some 378 congregations in the United States, should bring the congress and its 2,000 clergy and laymen delegates to Salt Lake City.

Reports at the congress reveal that the Greek Orthodox church is gaining in numbers, support and in development of church, educational and communal life facilities.

Like many other churches, the Greek Orthodox is laying particular emphasis on youth participation, a point stressed in a message to the congress from the Ecumenical Patriarch Athenagoras I of Constantinople.

In addition to reports and delegates' decisions on various questions of non doctrinal church policy, the congress will hear from such distinguished guest speakers as Ambassador George V. Melas of Greece and Howard W. Pyle, deputy assistant to President Eisenhower. Many distinguished Greek Orthodox Church leaders, including Archbishop Michael, primate of the Western Hemisphere, and the Most Reverend Metropolitan Germanos of Elias, Greece, are attending the sessions.

We trust the congress is in every way successful and that all those in attendance enjoy their visit to Salt Lake City and Utah.

—*Salt Lake Tribune*
July 2, 1958

Expansion in Ogden Beginning in the early 1950s, Greek parishioners in north Davis County and the Ogden area in Weber County wanted to establish a parish in Ogden. In 1956, John E. Papanikolas, Constantine J. Skedros, and Nick S. Vidalakis were appointed by the Salt Lake Parish Council to help Ogden parishioners find a suitable church location. In 1959, property at 674 42nd Street in South Ogden was purchased. Later, in 1962 the Transfiguration Greek Orthodox Church opened.

Helen Praggastis presides over this 1960 Greek school class. Among the students are Bill Rekouniotis, front row right; Jim Priskos, second row; Elias Koucos and John Luras, third row; John Koucos, fourth row and Leo Sotiriou and John Rice, back row.

Archbishop Iakovos consecrated the church on December 27–28, 1968. It was the third Greek Orthodox Church in Utah. Assisting the Archbishop were Fr. Simionidis, pastor of the Ogden church, and Fr. Elias Stephanopoulos, from Salt Lake City's Holy Trinity Church. More than 400 attended the historic service.

An agreement between the Salt Lake City and Ogden church groups designated the area north of Layton, including Ogden and Weber County, part of the new community. It was agreed, however, that parishioners could choose which church-community to support. Through the years a very close relationship continues to exist between the two churches.

1959

The Salt Lake community implemented one of the nation's first "Fair Share" membership programs to meet its budget needs. The program attracted more than 1,400 participants.

June 6: The general assembly voted to purchase two homes north of the Memorial Building for $29,000 for use as a parking lot.

The general assembly appointed a committee to evaluate the needs of the Sunday schools and the Greek schools. The committee of Nick G. Cozakos, Mike Kerikas, John Maragakis, Constantine J. Skedros, and John L. Strike recommended that the parish build additional classrooms in the Memorial Building and use the lower level of Holy Trinity Church for classrooms.

Board of Trustees Presidents: 1941–1962

Chris Tryfon, 1941	Ted J. Speros, 1954–1955
Alki T. Diamant, 1942	Nicholas L. Strike, 1956
John G. Condas, 1943	William G. Dokos, 1957
Paul Borovilos, 1944–1948	William D. Cocorinis, 1958
George Zeese, 1949–1950	Peter Vrontikis, 1959
Louis N. Strike, 1951	James G. Cayias, 1960
Peter S. Marthakis, 1952	John G. Papanikolas, 1961
James Velis, 1953	Nicholas Theos, 1962

Clergy: 1927–1962

The Rev. Stephanos Angelopoulos, 1927–1933
Archimandrite Artemios Stamatiadis, 1933–1935
The Rev. Harry Gavalas, 1935–1941
The Rev. John Vassiliadis, 1941–1944
The Rev. Antonios Kalogeropoulos, 1944–1954
The Rev. Angelo Gavalas, 1951–1952
The Rev. George Pulos, 1953–1955
The Rev. George Mestakides, 1955
The Rev. Steven A. Katsaris, 1955–1962
The Rev. James Adams, 1957–1960
The Rev. Leon Pachis, 1960–1962

The decade of the 1950s closed with triumph for the Greek Orthodox community of Salt Lake. Its example and influence spawned new churches in more and more viable and enthusiastic communities in the Intermountain region.

"When we were around 17, 18, 19 (years old) and girls were being married, a lot of marriages were still being fixed. There was a gal here and her mother and father tried to no end to get me to marry her. My mother would say, 'you know, she's got lots of property, you know her parents have a lot of money, you know and they'd deal.' I didn't like her. There was no way that I was going to marry her or anybody else on a fixed situation. But there were girls that did and they're (still) married today."

—Andy Katsanevas, b. 1922
Greek Oral History Collection

Holy Trinity Sunday School teachers gathered for this 1959–1960 photo included: Ted Poulos, back row left, Mary Bolaris, Vig Malkos, Goldie Rhinesmith, Bella Gaviotis, Mae Georgelas, Mary Adondakis, Mary Saltas Mannos, Kelly Chipian, Faye Sargent, Alice Katsanevas, and Presbytera Katsaris; middle row, Kay Koulis, left, Georgia Varanakis, Sylvia Varanakis, Sophie Saltas, Lula Rhodes, Viola Nicolatus, Wilma Savas, Georgia Georgiades, Irene Landures, Anna Pappas, Angie Bolic, and Mary Mastoris Mannos; front row, Mrs. Nick Royal, seated left, Sophie Loulias, Peter Loulias, Fr. James Adams, Fr. Steven A. Katsaris, Ted Sargent, and Diana Drake.

The ground-breaking ceremony for
Prophet Elias Church, September 30,
1968, was a major event, marking
the growth of the Salt Lake Greek
church-community. Rev. Elias
Stephanopoulos is at the
microphone and Utah Governor
Calvin Rampton, Bishop Meletios,
and Sam W. Souvall are among
those looking on.

Chapter 5

Controversy and Growth in the 1960s

During the 1960s, the Greek community focused on increasing participation in the Fair Share program. It also faced the choice of either building new Sunday school facilities at Holy Trinity or building a second church in the Salt Lake Valley.

In 1962, Fr. Steven A. Katsaris, who had served the parish since 1955, requested to be transferred and was assigned to the newly organized parish in Belmont, California. Fr. Katsaris had been instrumental in developing a new curriculum for the Sunday schools, was a catalyst for an increase in youth activities, and fostered strong spiritual growth in the parish. Fr. John Berris, whose assistant was Fr. Isaiah Chronopoulos, replaced him. Years later, Fr. Isaiah became Metropolitan of the Denver Diocese. (A Metropolitan ranks below an Archbishop and administers the nine Dioceses in the United States.)

In recognition of the continued growth of the community, the general assembly authorized a planning and advisory committee, in January 1963, to study all phases of church-community life, including the church constitution and bylaws, administration, finances, property acquisitions, current properties, church programs, and an additional church.

John Maragakis was chairman and Constantine J. Skedros secretary of the 40-person committee. After many meetings, various reports were prepared and submitted. The only positive actions to come from the committee's recommendations were the need to acquire properties north of Holy Trinity and to acquire property in the southeast area of Salt Lake County for a future church.

The community's uneasy relationship with the Archdiocese in New York created a problem in 1962–1964.

Happy Sunday school students respond to their teacher in this early 1960s photo.

The Salt Lake community had never accepted the constitution and bylaws of the Greek Orthodox Archdiocese of North and South America. The Salt Lake community's founding fathers and subsequent leaders were determined to remain independent from any ecclesiastical authority and control. But in the 1960s, many parishioners felt that they could no longer ignore the Archdiocese and accept its priests while remaining 100 percent independent. The issue was often debated in Parish Councils and in the general assemblies.

February 26–27, 1963: His Eminence Archbishop Iakovos made his first visitation to Salt Lake City. An elaborate celebration was held in his honor. He met with the Parish Council and other community leaders, pressing the need for the Salt Lake City church-community to accept the Archdiocese's constitution and bylaws. An overriding concern of the parish pertained to who would control the real property and funds of the local Greek community—the local parish or the Archdiocese in New York?

Throughout 1963, pressure from the Archdiocese to have the local parish join the Archdiocese increased markedly.

January 13–22, 1964: The University of Utah sponsored an event entitled "Spotlight on Greece" to promote international understanding and to further individual contact with the people of Greece. It featured Greek music, philosophy, sculpture, literature, and drama. Andre Michalopoulos, advisor to the Royal Greek Embassy, Washington D.C., presented the principal lecture at the university.

Archdiocese General Assembly

January 19, 1964: Bishop Demetrios from the Los Angeles Diocese and Fr. George Bacopoulos, Chancellor of the Greek Orthodox Archdiocese in New York City, attended a special general assembly to discuss the acceptance of the constitution of the Archdiocese. A very emotional and heated debate resulted in Bishop Demetrios and the clergy walking out of the assembly. But the arguments did not pertain solely to property ownership and fund ownership. There was a smaller but important local matter that needed to be resolved—that of allowing senior parish members full voting rights even though they did not pledge to pay the Archdiocese fee. After more negotiations, an agreement was reached on March 22, 1964. A special general assembly voted to accept the Archdiocese Uniform Parish Regulations and the Uniform Parish Bylaws with some exceptions.

Finally, the Salt Lake Greek church-community became part of the Greek Orthodox Archdiocese in New York City, but the local community retained total control over all real properties, funds, and property management. However, that same issue continues to fester in the Twenty-first Century.

Fr. Berris arrived in 1962 during a crucial period in the history of the parish. He was faced with the pressures of church expansion and with the task of continuing the work of Fr. Katsaris. Unfortunately, Fr. Berris became embroiled in community controversy and, as a result, became the center of criticism not entirely of his own doing. It must be noted that after his assistant, Fr. Isaiah, was transferred, Fr. Berris assumed the task of being the religious leader of the entire community without an assistant. It was at a time when accelerated growth of the Sunday school program and the pressure to build another church were major issues in the community.

Fr. Berris left Salt Lake City in March 1967, when he was transferred to San Jose, California. He served there nearly 20 years. Fr. Elias Stephanopoulos, who was then assigned to the Salt Lake parish, faced a divided community steeped in bitter feelings about the additional church and the transfer of Fr. Berris.

What had been discussed for years became obvious in 1960s: Sunday school facilities at Holy Trinity were woefully inadequate. The Parish Council considered plans to build a classroom wing on the Memorial Building, while many in the

The Parish Council of 1965 included George Adondakis, front left, and counter-clockwise John Chipian, George Papanikolas, Nick Sefakis, John Karpakis, Louis N. Strike, Fr. Mavridakis, Fr. John Berris, George Zeese, William Souvall, Louis Bovos, and George W. Papanikolas.

The Holy Trinity congretation filled the church in this 1960 photograph.

community wanted to either build another church or expand Holy Trinity. In February 1960, the parish planning committee was authorized to seek property in the southeast area of Salt Lake County for a new church complex. In June, 13 acres of land between 4600 and 4800 South and 1600 East were acquired, and a master plan for the proposed church was approved.

In 1965, anticipated enrollment for Sunday school classes was 1,000 youngsters. Many parishioners believed that the most viable solution to the Sunday school growth was an additional church. Some members believed this would divide the parish. Still others felt that such expansion would become an emotional issue, especially among the older parishioners who had worked hard to raise funds and build Holy Trinity in 1923–1925.

July 11, 1965: A special general assembly discussed three issues: the availability of property at Fort Douglas for a new church complex, the purchase of property at 5335 Highland

Drive for a new church complex, and the start of construction of a new church once funding became available.

After a lengthy and bitter debate, the following motion was presented to the membership: buy the property at 5335 Highland Drive and wait six months before taking action to see whether the Fort Douglas property would be available. If not, then the parish should proceed to build a church at the Highland Drive site.

Due to parliamentary technicalities, the motion was defeated. In protest to the delay in moving forward, 10 Parish Council members resigned: John Karpakis, Andy Panos, Nick Sefakis, George Adondakis, John Chipian, Wallace Jackson, Tony Kalevas, George W. Papanikolas, William Souvall, and George Zeese.

This led to a schism between those who wanted to build a second church and those who did not want to be rushed into making such a major decision. Within a few weeks, the Eastern Orthodox Progressives was organized. It advocated building the church immediately.

To keep the parish's business functioning, a re-organized Parish Council was formed, with Louis N. Strike, Andy Luras, Peter J. Poulos, Peter W. G. Cayias as officers. Board members were: Louis Bovos, Ernest Chipian, Alki T. Diamant, Mike Giamalakis, John Kotsovos, George J. Papanikolas, Nick Paras, Sam Rondas, Gus Sotiriou, Ted J. Speros, and John L. Strike.

1965–1968

August 1965: The reorganized Parish Council agreed to upgrade the Sunday school facilities by adding 10 classrooms to the Memorial Building. The council also agreed to sell the church-owned property at 4600 South 1600 East and to conduct a study to determine the best location for the proposed church. The latter task was given to a committee consisting of Andy Luras, Thano Castles, John Kumarelas, and Constantine J. Skedros.

November 1965: Some unity was restored among the various factions and plans began to move slowly forward after

---

"Downtown (Salt Lake City) we (his brother William and his partner) had a pool hall, high class pool hall. Doctors and lawyers and business come in and played. It was very clean place. So these fellows run another pool hall further up (the street) and they got jealous and they sent Jack Dempsey down to make a noise and break the place. That was six months before he became (heavyweight boxing) champion of the world. So Jack Dempsey come around and throw the balls here and I go over to correct it and he says 'Get the hell out of here.' Vokopulos' (the partner) father, he was sitting upstairs and this door was open, you know, and he heard that and he come down and grabbed Jack Dempsey and throw him upstairs on the rails. That's how strong he was."

—George Cayias, b. 1896
Greek Oral History Collection

Members of the 5335 Building Committee, which was to supervise all aspects of a new church included John Maragakis, standing left, Sam W. Souvall, Jim Kastanis, Contantine J. Skedros, George Furgis; Stella Maverakis, seated left, Fr. Elias Stephanopoulos, Fr. George Stephanopoulos, and John Billinis.

a special general assembly when the construction of the new classrooms was approved. At a general assembly the following spring, it was decided overwhelmingly to buy property at 5335 South Highland Drive for a new church, and to sell the property at 4600 Highland Drive, valued at $130,000. In May of 1966, the community bought the first of several parcels of property at 5335 South Highland Drive for $35,000.

February 24, 1966: The University of Utah's Pioneer Memorial Theater honored Alexander Matsos, Ambassador

of Greece, at its premiere performance of "Oedipus Rex." He visited Utah at the invitation of the Utah Symphony Guild in response to the Utah Symphony Orchestra's invitation to play in the Athens Festival to be held the following September.

1967: Unity prevailed and the newly elected Parish Council moved forward with Sam W. Souvall as president. He emphasized the need to re-establish unity and goodwill within the community, begin preliminary work on a new church on Highland Drive, resolve issues involving the clergy, and organize a major fund-raising drive for the building program.

A 5335 Building Committee was appointed and given the responsibility to supervise the planning, funding, and construction of a new church complex that was to serve the entire Greek community. Members of this committee were George Furgis and Sam W. Souvall, co-chairmen, and board members Bill Alexander, George Adondakis, John Billinis, John Maragakis, George Nicolatus, Constantine J. Skedros, Ted J. Speros, Nick L. Theos, and Nick S. Vidalakis, who was to organize and direct fundraising.

The committee later added Parish Council presidents Nick Sefakis, Jim Kastanis, Andy Katsanevas, Philoptochos Society presidents Stella Maverakis and Mary C. Giannopulos, and Fr. Stephanopoulos.

February 25, 1967: Louis N. Strike was honored at a testimonial dinner held in the Memorial Building and sponsored by the Salt Lake Area Chamber of Commerce and the Holy Trinity Greek Orthodox community. In recognition of his achievements, he was awarded the Chamber of Commerce First Citizen Award. Principle speakers were Utah's Governor Calvin Rampton and United States Senator Wallace F. Bennett.

April 1968: The concept of a united community with a single Parish Council was advanced. Parish members unanimously voted that any attempt or motion in a special general assembly to divide the Greater Salt Lake Greek Orthodox Community would require a minimum of six-month's written notice, general assembly discussion, and a minimum vote of 300—or 75 percent of the total eligible membership of the parish.

September 30, 1968: With more than $500,000 pledged during fundraising, groundbreaking took place at the 5335 Highland Drive site. The children of the late Louis (Elias) and Christina Chipian Strike—Nicholas, Kay, John, and George—having made a substantial pledge to the new church, were accorded naming rights. The church was named "Prophet Elias" in memory of their father.

August 24, 1969: Archbishop Iakovos conducted the "Opening Doors" service at Prophet Elias Church, which was still under construction. The first liturgy was held on December 21, 1969.

Soon, it was decided that a choir should serve at Prophet Elias Church and that the main church-community office would remain at Holy Trinity. Parents would select which church they would attend and their children would be enrolled at that church's Sunday school. The clergy would rotate every other Sunday between the two churches. The committee agreed that *one* Parish Council would manage the affairs of the two churches.

Initially, cost of the new church was estimated to be $762,000 but more work was needed before it could be declared complete. In 1970, the cost of land, building, and furnishings was estimated to be $900,000.

January 1968: The Parish Council voted to hire Fr. George Stephanopoulos, the father of its current priest, Fr. Elias, to serve as his assistant. That move facilitated the

---

"…see, the reason I left to Logan… there was a lot of Greek boys in here and if I stay here I never will learn any English… and after that if somebody told me, why don't you go to Logan? Nice little town, no Greeks in there.

So I went to Logan. I got a job in an Eagle Hotel which was Logan Hotel… and I stay with a wonderful family… Mr. and Mrs. Whitney."

—George Lamb, b. 1891
Greek Oral History Collection

beginning of having two Divine Liturgies, the first in Greek and the second in Greek and English. The reason for the two liturgies was to serve the large number of people attending services, including Sunday school children.

1968–1969

1968: The concept of establishing the Hellenic St. Luke Home for Senior Citizens gained favor and efforts were made to acquire property east and adjoining Holy Trinity Church (the La France Apartments). Two parishioners, Vasiliki Lambros, Magna, and Peter Loulias, Midvale, donated real

estate to the parish. Funds from the sale of these properties were earmarked for the senior citizens' home.

1969: The storied Black Rock Beach Resort on the southern shores of Great Salt Lake, developed in the 1930s by the late James Latsis and his wife, Virginia Latsis Zamboukos, was put up for sale. At her request, the Parish Council agreed to assist Mrs. Zamboukos with the sale of her property. In 1980 she bequeathed $65,000 to the Greek community.

August 23–28: The Salt Lake community was the host for the 18th International Greek Orthodox Youth of America (GOYA) Conference. Archbishop Iakovos and several

Director Paul Maritsas, seated front center, and the Prophet Elias choir in an early 1980's photo.

hundred delegates, visitors, and clergy from parishes throughout the country attended. A conference highlight was the "Sounds of Interfaith" program, staged in the Salt Lake Tabernacle on Temple Square on August 25, 1969. Main speakers were Archbishop Iakovos, Marion Hanks of the Council of Twelve Apostles of the Church of Jesus Christ of Latter-day Saints, and Rev. Dr. Stanley Harakas, professor at the Holy Cross School of Theology, Brookline, Massachusetts. Also offering remarks were Utah Governor Calvin Rampton, and U.S. Senators from Utah, Wallace F. Bennett and Frank Moss. The Holy Trinity Choir also performed. The conference was under the leadership of Harry Pappasideris, Mike Adondakis, George Miller, Joanne Saltas, and Maria Nicolatus.

Clergy: 1962–1975

The Rev. John Berris, 1962–1967
The Rev. Isaiah Chronopoulos, 1962–1964
The Rev. Elias Stephanopoulos, 1967–1975
The Rev. George Stephanopoulos, 1968–1974
The Rev. Steven Prodromides, 1972–1974

A new church, a united community, two Divine Liturgies, expanded youth programs, and resourceful fundraising and service programs marked the achievements of the Greek-community in the turbulent 1960s.

Planners for the Greek Orthodox Youth Association conference in Salt Lake City in 1969 included Estelle Speros, left, Roger Haran, Nina Cutrubis, Diana Tuzios, and Harry Pappasideris.

"When we were having hard times during the Depression and after that time, this owner of the grocery store gave us better rent. At that time we had our three children. Many times in those days we ate bread, olives, radishes and sandwiches so we could save and not close the business. We did not have much business during that time."

—Adelina Burascano Lingos
Greek Oral History Collection

85

Gathered for a photograph after presentation of the St. Paul Award for Service to Church and Community in 1971, were William D. Cocorinis, left, Angie L. Chipian, Stella Maverakis, Nick S. Vidalakis, Fr. George Stephanopoulos, Nick Cozakos, Archbishop Iakovos, Fr. Geranios, Presbytera Anastasia Stephanopoulos, Fr. Elias Stephanopoulos, Helen Zeese Papanikolas, Nicholas L. Strike, Andy Katsanevas, and Peter Loulias.

Chapter 6

Community Growth in the 1970s

The decade of the 1970s was marked by expansion. The parish's real estate committee, Nick S. Vidalakis, Constantine J. Skedros, and Nick Theos, recommended the purchase of the Covey Apartments, also known as the La France, east of Holy Trinity on 300 South. The Parish Council approved the recommendation, acknowledging the cost to be $610,000, and the vote to purchase was favorable. Later in 1970, the Parish Council renewed the option to purchase the apartments. A certified appraisal valued the property at $280,000, and it was bought for that amount on May 28, 1972.

Holy Trinity Church interior.

The down payment came from funds earmarked for St. Luke's senior citizens' home and from the sale of donated properties in Magna and Midvale. The intent was to make some units available to Greek senior citizens. The mortgage was paid off in 1990 and income derived from rental of the apartments has been added to the church budget.

1970s

During the period of the 1970s–1980s, a group of students from Greece and Cyprus were attending the University of Utah. Many were graduate-degree candidates. Through the efforts of Salt Lake City attorney and Greek community activist Nick Colessides, the Society of Greek

Students and Professionals was organized and it functioned for several years.

Spring 1970: Two highly acclaimed and well-researched works, "Toil and Rage in a New Land" and "The Greek Immigrants of Utah," by Helen Zeese Papanikolas, were published by the *Utah State Historical Quarterly* (Volume No. 38). In 1972, she became the editor of a state bicentennial project, *The Peoples of Utah*, that highlighted Utah's ethnic groups, including a chapter on the Greeks. For her outstand-

ing work, she was honored as "Fellow of Utah History" and was chosen to serve on the Utah State Board of History.

Early 1970: The Tonelli Art Studios of Chicago, Illinois, were contracted to install the mosaics for the Platetera and the Pantokrator at Prophet Elias Church. The Sam W. Souvall family donated $43,000 for that project.

September 1970: Fr. Steven Prodromides was assigned to the Salt Lake parish as assistant priest. His main area of service, beyond his duties as a clergyman, was working with the youth.

December 1971: The parish hosted the quarterly meeting of the Archdiocesan Council. Archbishop Iakovos presented the St. Paul Award for service to the church and the community to parish members Angie Chipian, William D. Cocorinis, Nick Cozakos, Andy Katsanevas, Peter Loulias, Stella Maverakis, Helen Zeese Papanikolas, and Nicholas L. Strike. This was the first time Salt Lake parishioners were so honored. The medal of St. Paul is awarded by the Greek Holy Archdiocese of America for service to the church and community and is the highest honor a lay person can receive in this country.

March 1972: As part of its Greek Independence Day activities the community honored native son, Tom C. Korologos, Washington, D.C., who served as banquet keynote speaker. Korologos was born and raised in Salt Lake City, son of Greek immigrant parents, Chris and Irene Korologos, who operated a bar called The Bomb Shelter in the downtown

Opa! Ellen Kounalis, front left, Nick Varanakis, Mercy Vassiliades, Terry Chipian, and John Varanakis posed during a 1970's activity.

area. At the time of his visit, Korologos was special assistant to President Richard M. Nixon. Later he served in the White House under President Gerald R. Ford. In 1988, the University of Utah honored Korologos with a Distinguished Alumni Award and with an honorary doctorate in June 2003. After a career as a lobbyist in Washington, Korologos was appointed U.S. Ambassador to Belgium in June 2004.

April 1972: A request from parishioner George Politis to enter the priesthood as lay priest was accepted by the Parish Council and forwarded to the Archdiocese, which had a program that allowed qualified individuals to be ordained as lay priests to help mitigate the serious shortage of clergy. In 1972, he was the first layman in Salt Lake City to be ordained as a priest.

1972: Nick Metalinos, a University of Utah student and well-known performer of Greek dancing, offered his talents and expertise to help organize the first dance group, the Dionysus Dancers. Metalinos and several other parishioners also organized the Greek American Cultural Center of Salt Lake City. It followed the Hellenic Cultural Society of Utah, which was organized in 1971. Thus, the community boasted two cultural groups with the goal of preserving Greek culture. University of Utah adjunct professor and Salt Lake businessman, William D. Cocorinis, and Harry Anstall, a physician, headed the Hellenic Cultural Society of Utah. Other members included Constantine J. Skedros, John Billinis, Nick G. Cozakos, Tim Folias, Paul Maritsas, and Nick Colessides.

October 28, 1972: The Greek American Cultural Center, under the direction of Metalinos, presented a program commemorating the events that led to "OXI " (NO) Day in 1940 during the war between Greece and Italy. The group also presented a program on December 2, 1972, honoring the memory of George Seferis, Greece's Nobel Prize winner in literature.

First Greek Candidate for Governor

In the spring of 1972, Nicholas L. Strike, past president of the Greek community and a well-known civic leader and business executive, became a candidate for governor of Utah on the Republican ticket. Governor Calvin Rampton (D), who was re-elected to an unprecedented third term, defeated him. Strike's nomination was a significant achievement for a member of Utah's Greek-American community.

Clergy Problems Persist During 1972, a controversy arose over the duties of the father-son team of Frs. George and Elias Stephanopoulos, who were serving in the Greek community. On May 31, the Parish Council confronted them with 13 allegations regarding their work schedules, hospital visitations and, in general terms, their relationships with some parishioners. The clergy defended their activities and no other action was taken.

The Parish Council voted 6 to 4 on November 28, 1972 to terminate the employment of the two priests effective January 1, 1973. The Archdiocese was informed, but took no action. Unfortunately, minutes of several Parish Council meetings and general assemblies of that period are missing and an official account is not available.

January 16, 1973: The Parish Council voted 10 to 4 to request the Archdiocese to immediately transfer Fr. Elias Stephanopoulos. At the meeting, Fr. Elias asked the Parish Council to inform the parishioners about issues but the council took no such action. A few days later, Fr. George Bacopoulos, the Chancellor of the Archdiocese, arrived in Salt Lake City to investigate the situation. He told the council that the Archbishop would decide if and when Fr. Elias would be transferred.

February 2, 1973: Archbishop Iakovos notified the council that he would transfer Fr. Elias during the summer. The council voted 10 to 5 to inform the Archdiocese that it wanted Fr. Elias reassigned by June 1, 1973.

Simultaneously, a petition, sponsored by supporters of Fr. Elias, began to circulate in the parish. It called for a special general assembly to rescind the transfer request.

"My husband's uncle came to my dad and he says, I got a boy for your daughter…and my father come home at night and he says to me, he know I was kind of miffed with my stepmother. I can't get along with her, you know, and he says, I got somebody come up today and told me. He seems nice boy. Not far from our home town. I say okay.

"…Well I was engaged with him. And my dad have a few friends and they told him. One of them…wants me to marry his brother…Not because it was me but because the Greek ladies, they didn't come…then my dad says, you're not going to marry Tom. He says, you're going to marry this fellow. And I says, if I'm not going to marry Tom, I'm not going to marry anybody. He says, no you're going to get married to the other fellow, not Tom. So I got mad one day and I eloped…That was a very small wedding. Just the two of us and three more people…Got married at the Greek church, the first one, it was at 5th West and 5th South, someplace down there."

—Helen Ioannou Kannes, b. 1907
Greek Oral History Collection

The high-jumping, knee-slapping Dionysus Dancers are Greek Festival entertainment favorites. This is a 1996 Dionysus Dance Group.

In March, the Parish Council voted not to recognize the petition's request to convene a general assembly because the council considered such a meeting invalid. Instead, the council decided to hold a regular general assembly on April 15. That did not appease the petitioners who continued with their plans to hold an assembly on April 1. They felt that their request for a special session was valid and legal and that the Parish Council did not have the right to deny their request.

April 1, 1973: The largest attendance of any general or special assembly up to that time 472 parishioners—gathered. Nick Colessides and Gus J. Anton presented a resolution urging "…the Archdiocese and Archbishop Iakovos to rescind the decision of reassigning Father Elias Stephanopoulos…"

The resolution passed, 396 to 6, with 10 abstentions. Then the special general assembly appointed a committee to carry out the resolution's intent. Members were John Kelaidis, president of the Parish Council; William D. Cocorinis, member of the Archdiocesan Council; Nicholas L. Strike, member of the Archdiocesan Council; and John Billinis and Stella Maverakis, representing the parish.

But peace was not to be—yet. Two weeks later, at the regularly scheduled general assembly, council president Kelaidis, presented the council's objection to the actions and assembly meeting held on April 1. That regular assembly resolved:

> "…that the four attorneys present: Nick Colessides, Alki T. Diamant, Harry Metos and Mark Theodore, having met prior to the start of the general assembly and after examining the Uniform Parish By-Laws, have concluded that the Special General Assembly of April 1, 1973, was properly and legally constituted as pursuant to the rules and regulations of the parish."

After a lengthy discussion, the following motion was overwhelmingly approved:

> "That the General Assembly of April 15, 1973, re-affirms all the proceedings and motions of the Special General Assembly of April 1, 1973."

At this juncture, 11 members of the Parish Council resigned and walked out of the assembly: John Kelaidis, John Chipian, Jim Davis, Gus Daskalakis, Pan Doudaniotis, Jim Funtas, Andy Katsanevas, Harry Pappasideris, Bill Thomas Peters, Paul Roumpos, and Sakis Sakellariou. Soon thereafter, Fr. Elias and William D. Cocorinis, as the parish's representatives to the Archdiocesan Council, appointed new members to the parish's governing council. They were: Gus E. Papanikolas, president; Nick S. Vidalakis, vice president; Vickie Folias, secretary, and Paul Liapis, a holdover board member, as treasurer. Constituting the board were John Billinis, Cocorinis, Mike Giamalakis, Alex Kralios M.D., Andy Luras (holdover), George E. Mantes, John Maragakis, Gregory J. Skedros, Gus Vetas (holdover), and Michael Zervos (holdover).

December 1974: Archbishop Iakovos informed the Parish Council that he was constantly receiving letters from Salt Lake City stating that Fr. Elias was trying to divide the community. The Archbishop suggested that a change in assignment for Fr. Elias might be necessary.

In the spring of 1975, Fr. Elias formally requested the Archdiocese to transfer him after the Parish Council had approved his request. Fr. George Stephanopoulos had retired in March 1974.

Fr. Elias was assigned to the Holy Trinity Greek Orthodox Church in Portland, Oregon, in June 1975, where he served until his death in 1994. He had arrived in Salt Lake City in March 1967, when the community was divided on the issue of building a second church. Through his efforts, the parish came together and the construction of Prophet Elias Church became a reality.

1974

The parish's annual payment of the Archdiocese obligation, both current and $22,000 that was past due, troubled the parish at the beginning of 1974. William D. Cocorinis negotiated with the Archdiocese and the parish's 1974 obligation was written off in exchange for a promise that the 1975 assessment of $24,000 would be paid.

A major fund-raising event called MPO for Mortgage Payoff and aimed at paying off the mortgage on Prophet Elias was held at the Terrace Ballroom. It netted $170,000.

March 13: Los Angeles County Sheriff Peter J. Pitchess received a Distinguished Alumni Award from the University of Utah Alumni Association. He was recognized for his distinguished career in law enforcement that began in 1940. Pitchess was born in 1912 to Greek immigrant parents and reared in Salt Lake City and Bingham Canyon. After graduating from the University of Utah College of Law in 1940, he served with the Federal Bureau of Investigation and later as sheriff of Los Angeles County for 24 years. His wife was the former Athena Takis, also a Salt Lake City native.

Fall: Salt Lake Greek-American Nick Zolintakis was defeated in the primary round in his bid to be Salt Lake County treasurer.

1975

First Sunday School Graduation

May 29: A dinner honored the graduating class and faculty of the parish Sunday schools. May Gooras and her sister, Kay Koulis, presented Bibles to 22 seniors. That was the first of a now-annual presentation made in memory of Lazarus and Steven Gooras, father and uncle of the sisters. Later, the George Kampros family began the practice of donating Bibles to the graduates in memory of their parents, George and Vig Kampros. Peter Loulias was superintendent of the schools, with Nick Cozakos directing Holy Trinity activities and George Tsalaky overseeing the Prophet Elias program. The graduation festivities were co-chaired by Vig Kampros and Anna K. Skedros.

"Well, the service of our church used to be long but had to be because the monasteries where they got the monks, that's the way they had to do it. And after Greece was liberated from the Turks, they started getting shorter, even maybe they sometimes they going to shorten it so it won't be more than between three-quarters of an hour to an hour. Now they go from an hour and 15 minutes for the liturgy and they got orthos. I don't know how to call it."

—Paul Borovilos
Greek Oral History Collection

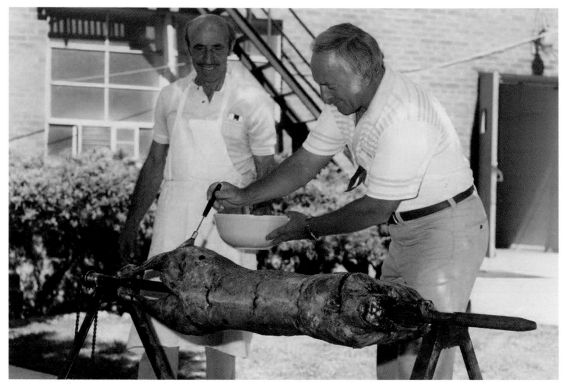
In 1980, George Kardaras, left, and Jim Kastanis prepared the Greek Festival's roasted lamb.

July 28: The Greek American Cultural Association presented a Greek Folk Dancing Concert directed by Nick Metalinos. The program was a farewell tribute to Nick and Barbara Metalinos who were leaving Salt Lake City. Since 1972, the couple had been instrumental in establishing a Greek folk-dance program. Since then, Greek folk-dance programs have become an important cultural and community outreach phenomenon and are a highlight of the annual Greek Festival.

As a result of the efforts of Helen Zeese Papanikolas in 1975, the Holy Trinity Greek Orthodox Church was placed in the National and State Registers of Historic Places.

First Greek Festival

The Hellenic Mothers' Club, and its successor, the Philoptochos Society, had been holding fund-raising bazaars for several years. In 1975, Gregory J. and Jenny Skedros rallied the entire church-community to put on the first Greek Festival by combining the Philoptochos Bazaar and the community's car raffle in October with this letter:

Announcing Salt Lake's First Greek Festival
October 25 and 26, 1975

Each year the Greek community of Salt Lake City sponsors a car raffle as its major fund-raising event. The proceeds from this, I feel, subsidize the general budget for the entire year. As startling as it may seem to you, the 1973 car raffle netted the community only $1,000 and the 1974 car raffle netted a meager $500.

Our fair share membership dues and a few small fundraising efforts are usually adequate to meet the demand of our basic budget, but each year other important projects that are necessary are neglected due to the poor financial status of our church.

For example: The flooding of the basement of Prophet Elias has become critical and we are now faced with a possible expense of $20,000 to correct the situation, the beautiful electronic carillons of Holy Trinity have been out of commission for many years, and the kitchen at Holy Trinity does not even meet the basic requirements of the Salt Lake Board of Health. These are just three classic examples, of many, that illustrate the growing need of funds beyond the budget demands.

Obviously the need for genuine efforts towards fundraising activities becomes very apparent. Consequently, this year we are making a first attempt at what we hope to be an annual community sponsored affair. The Greek community car raffle and the Philoptochos Bazaar will be combined and all efforts will be directed towards our first annual community sponsored "GREEK FESTIVAL."

Enclosed you will find 12 raffle tickets at a cost of $1.50 each with a total value of $18.00. The price to you will be $15.00 with two free tickets. All ticket stubs that are to be deposited must be paid for in advance.

In order for this new venture to be an outstanding success, it must truly be a community effort. Very soon many of you will be called upon for donations and to accept various committee assignments. If all of us either purchases or sells his raffle tickets, we can be assured that the first "GREEK FESTIVAL" will be a great success!

Sincerely,

Gregory J. Skedros, Chairman
Fund-raising Committee

1976–1978

1976: The parish requested a $200,000 grant from the Utah State Historical Society and the State Preservation Office to help restore and protect the stained glass windows at Holy Trinity Church. A portion of the request was funded and the parish raised the additional money.

December 1976: The Crane property at 240 South 200 West (now 300 West) Street was bought by the community for $125,000. It was purchased from Salt Lake businessman Sam Skaggs, who told parishioner Sam W. Souvall that he would donate $20,000 to the church if it purchased the property by December 31, 1976. Since the purchase, the 52,000 square-foot property has been leased to Crane Building tenants for parking, with income going to the church.

January 10, 1977: A Memorial Building Committee, consisting of Peter W. Souvall, Sam Chelemes, George Melissas, Andy Katsanevas, and James P. Pappas, was appointed to plan for expansion of the Hellenic Memorial Building. The project included adding a dining area with a seating capacity of 400, expanding the kitchen, and adding church offices and storage space on a second floor. Construction on the so-called memorial building "Annex" in the spring of 1977 found up to 25 members of the parish volunteering 10–12 hours on weekends to try to finish the building by Greek Festival time in September. The expansion cost approximately $125,000.

April 24, 1977: The general assembly approved creation of a Greater Salt Lake Greek Orthodox Foundation for ongoing financial benefit to the community. Committee members were Sam W. Souvall, Nick S. Vidalakis, Nick Colessides, George Furgis, and Peter W. Souvall. In addition, Constantine J. Skedros was named chairman of a Long-range Planning Committee.

1977: Capital improvement projects for Holy Trinity Church and Prophet Elias Church were on the community's

Gregory J. Skedros and his wife Jenny co-chaired first Greek Festival.

agenda. Holy Trinity required a new icon screen, pulpit, bishop's throne, chanter's stand, and icon stands in the Narthex. Prophet Elias Church requirements included the Pantokrator, the Platetera, pulpit, and chanter's stand. George Furgis chaired fundraising.

May 1978: The Philoptochos Society sponsored a luncheon in the Hellenic Memorial Building. It honored nearly 100 senior citizens of the community, all of them natives of Greece. *The Salt Lake Tribune* reported as follows:

Greek Orthodox Seniors Honored

One-hundred-year-old John Mantas topped a list of distinguished guests at a luncheon Wednesday where the Philoptochos Society of the Salt Lake Area Greek Orthodox Churches honored nearly 100 senior citizen members.

In addition to the oldest member, the philanthropic organization presented gifts to Steve and John Zervos, 97 and 96 years old, respectively. Mr. and Mrs. George Zeese received a special honor for being married 65 years, and Mrs. Zeese also was recognized as being past president of the church's Mother's Club.

According to chairman Mrs. John Kelaidis, this was the first time the church's seniors were honored. The luncheon, at the Hellenic Memorial Bldg., 279 South 300 West, was held in conjunction with Senior Citizen's Month.

Other couples married for more than 50 years who received gifts were Mr. and Mrs. Gus Delis, 64 years; Mr. and Mrs. Louis Lingos, 60; Mr. and Mrs. John Zekas, 58; Mr. and Mrs. John Mantas, 55; Mr. and Mrs. Emanuel Ladakis, 55; Mr. and Mrs. Jim Souvall, 55; Mr. and Mrs. Peter Demiris, 56; Mr. and Mrs. Pete Pappas, 65; Mr. and Mrs. Peter Souvall, 52; and Mr. and Mrs. George Mihalopulos, 50 years.

The luncheon also cited the oldest Parish Council president, Ernie Chipian, who was president in 1931. Other past presidents recognized were Mr. Zeese, John Kotsovos, George Papanikolos, and Paul Borovilos.

Other past Mother's Club presidents honored were Maria Takis, Tula Giannopulos, and Eugenia Ypsilantis. And the club also honored Virginia Latsis Zamboukos, Maria Takis and Kiki Skedros.

Most of the gifts presented, said Mrs. Kelaidis, consisted of bottles of champagne, wine, house plants and fruit baskets.

The "senior" senior citizen, Mr. Mantas, is a former employee of the Hogle Zoo for 25 years and supervised the breeding of a male tiger and female lion, which resulted in the birth of Shasta, the only know liger in captivity.

—Salt Lake Tribune
May 1978

May 1978: William Kandas of Minot, North Dakota, was appointed community executive director.

August 6, 1978: The Parish Council authorized the purchase of two pieces of property north of the Hellenic Memorial Building, at 235 South 300 West (for $40,500), and at 247 South 300 West (for $55,000).

• A summer program for preschool and elementary school children was launched in 1978, as a result of previous discussions about the establishment of a Greek Orthodox preschool at Prophet Elias Church. A committee, consisting of Elaine Bapis, Maria Pappasideris, Vickie Folias, Harry Anstall, Nick Mihalopoulos, and Bill Drossos, was instrumental in the school's opening.

June 1978: The Western States Choir Federation conference attracted numerous church choirs from the western part of the United States. The national convention of the Pan Cretan Association of America drew several hundred attendees. As a result of this convention's success, the combined Cretan organizations of the area, in 1980, donated $25,000 for a mosaic of Prophet Elias that was placed in the entrance to Prophet Elias Church.

1979: The church received a donation from Alki and Mary Diamant that was earmarked to renovate Holy Trinity Church's Iconostasion, which was part of the original Holy Trinity Church built in 1905.

Greek Festival-goers in 1996, get into the rhythm as they watch the dance groups perform.

Parish Council Presidents: 1963–1980

James G. Cayias, 1963	*Bill Thomas Peters, 1972*
William Legeros, 1964	*John Kelaidis, 1973*
Louis N. Strike, 1965	*Gus E. Papanikolas, 1973*
George C. Furgis, 1966	*William Cocorinis, 1974–1975*
Sam W. Souvall, 1967	*Peter W. Souvall, 1976–1977*
Nick Sefakis, 1968	*James P. Pappas, 1978–1979*
Jim Kastanis, 1969	*Harry Anstall M.D., 1980*
Andy Katsanevas, 1970–71	

• The Greater Salt Lake Greek community's vision for expanded facilities and services, and its creative efforts to fund the necessary improvements, exhibited exemplary commitment on the part of parish members. It laid the groundwork for greater achievements to come in the remaining decades of the Twentieth Century.

Prophet Elias Church has served Greek Orthodox worshippers since 1969. The construction of this second church alleviated over-crowding problems at Holy Trinity Church.

Chapter 7

An Era of Cultural Contributions

The growth of Greek-community organizations, programming, church beautification, property purchased for future expansion, and overcoming parish and clerical challenges with faith and persistence had set the tone for greater growth in the 1980s and 1990s. That growth would make memorable cultural contributions well beyond the confines of the Orthodox communities.

Prophet Elias iconostasion.

The community's 75th anniversary festivities included the annual Greek Independence Day banquet, which honored George C. Furgis for his efforts in raising funds for the completion of Prophet Elias and restoration work at Holy Trinity Church. A banquet at Little America Hotel featured speeches by Nick Colessides and Constantine J. Skedros, and a play, "A New Beginning," directed by Paul Maritsas.

1980

A summer day camp for children was launched under the direction of Fr. Dean Gigicos, with the assistance of Elaine Bapis, Vickie Folias, Vickie Peters, and Stephanie Chachas. More than 125 young people participated. It was followed by another program, the Summer Bible School, which continues today, unlike the summer day-camp program, which ended in 1983.

• Extensive basement remodeling at Holy Trinity was completed due, in large part, to a generous donation from Diamond Miles. The Philoptochos Society donated money to build a bride's room as part of the remodel project.

• A group of young Greek Orthodox students at the University of Utah, with the support of Fr. Dean Gigicos and Fr. Emanuel Lillios, organized the Eastern Orthodox Christian Student Organization. Its purpose was to establish and cultivate an awareness and understanding of Eastern Orthodox Christianity at the university through weekly lectures and vesper services. Some of the organizers were Andrew Pippas, Dean Athens, Mark Kouris, Greg Macris, Denise Pappas, James C. Skedros, and John G. Skedros. By 1985, some 50 orthodox students were involved. Criticized by Fr. Andrew Mahalares, who had replaced Fr. Gigicos as head priest, the group eventually ceased to function.

"And Greeks have a way about marriage. To them it is an important thing. Their philosophy is that out of the three main events in your life, birth, marriage, death, you only control one, which is marriage.

"...When my dad got married in 1913 he put an ad in the paper, the Bingham Bulletin, *inviting the whole city...and, oh, he had about 40 lambs. They barbecued them all."*

—George Condas, b. 1914
Greek Oral History Collection

Prophet Elias Mosaics Several sections of the mosaic from the Pantokrator at Prophet Elias Church fell from the ceiling on May 12, 1981. Because other sections of the Platetera were loose and in danger of falling, the church was closed and remained so for nearly two years. Church services were held in the adjacent recreation hall during this period. Andrew Katsanevas, Bill Kandas, and James Cayias set out to determine why the mosaics had fallen. There were allegations of poor workmanship.

During 1981, Mary Diamant, Bill Kandas, Andy Katsanevas, and Bruce Shand worked with the insurance company and the Pittsburgh Testing Laboratory to try to resolve the problem of the mosaics at Prophet Elias. In 1983, negotiations with the insurance company proved successful when a settlement for $120,000 was reached. Of that amount, $40,000 went to an outside law firm and $80,000 was placed in the Mosaic Restoration Fund. In 1989, the Parish Council unanimously approved an agreement with Sirio Tonelli Art Studios that would replace the Pantokrator, repair damaged sections of the Platetera, and install additional mosaics. The community would pay $90,000 and the studios would assume the balance of the work expense estimated to be $150,000.

1982

- The name of the Hellenic Memorial Building was changed to the Hellenic Memorial Cultural Center.

- "The Greek Exhibit," sponsored by an organization called The Peoples of Utah under the leadership of Helen Zeese Papanikolas, opened at the Utah State Historical Society Museum. The exhibit portrayed the experiences and life of the early Greek immigrants in Utah and featured artifacts that Mrs. Papanikolas had obtained from many individuals. It was visited by thousands of people during the three years it was on display. In May of 1992, portions of the exhibit became a focal point of the Hellenic Cultural Museum exhibit in the lower level of Holy Trinity Church.

- Contributions to the Fair Share Program were markedly less than expected. In November, the Parish Council decided to alter the fund-raising approach and begin a new stewardship campaign in 1983.

- The Parish Council established the Archives and Historical Committee and charged it with preserving the historical records of the church-community dating back to the time the first Greek immigrants arrived in Salt Lake City. The committee consisted of: Thano Castles, Nick Mihalopoulos, John Chipian, Chris Metos, Louis J. Cononelos, Helen Zeese Papanikolas, Janeen Costa, James P. Pappas, John Delis, Steve Sargetakis, Helen Demetropolis, Constantine J. Skedros, Mary Diamant, Lucretia Watkins, Mike Katsanevas, Sandra Fuller, Andy Katsanevas, Penelope Koulouris, and Fr. Lillios. In 1986, the Hellenic Cultural Association assumed the historical preservation duties.

Parish Council Presidents: 1981–1992

Mary Diamant, 1981
Constantine J. Skedros, 1982–1983
James G. Cayias, 1984–1985
George J. Cayias, 1986
Peter W. Souvall, 1987–1989
Stan Kouris, 1990
Sam Chelemes, 1991–1992

1983

- The community bought the Richards properties, located north of Holy Trinity Church, for $300,000. Money for the down payment was provided by: Diamond Miles donation, $60,000; Greek Festival 1982, $25,000; Greek Festival 1983, $33,000, and the estate of Jack Tallas, $2,000.

- The Redevelopment Agency of Salt Lake City offered assistance to the community in the hope that it would expedite the renovation of the La France Apartments and adjacent cottages and bring them up to minimum building codes. The offer was for a loan of $425,000 at five-percent interest. The Parish Council decided it would continue to make necessary repairs on the apartment units without the loan.

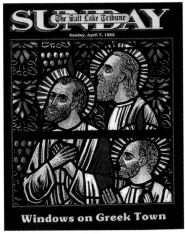

Windows on Greek Town, photograph and article from the *Salt Lake Tribune*, April 7, 1985.

The Greek community's Olympic Float, entered in the 1984 Days of '47 Parade, won the Salt Lake City Mayor's Award for "Best Community Float."

Parish Responds to Challenges

1984

A conflict developed between Fr. Andrew Mahalares and Fr. George Politis pertaining to, among other things, the part-time employment status of Fr. Politis. The rift resulted in Fr. Politis submitting his resignation, an action not favored by the Parish Council. Casualties of this internal conflict resulted in the termination of the summer programs for preschoolers and other young children of the parish.

Even though issues involving the priests were resolved by Bishop Anthimos of Denver, four Parish Council members, Maxine Babalis, Mike G. Makris, Gus Colessides, and John Shilaos, resigned. In January of 1985, Fr. Mahalares assumed responsibility for the resignations of Parish Council members as well as the divisive issues that had developed among the clergy. With that announcement he wanted to put the conflicts in the past and move the parish ahead peacefully.

January: A committee, under the chairmanship of James P. Pappas, was appointed to determine the feasibility of building a Senior Citizens' Living Center. On May 14, the committee of Constantine J. Skedros, Ellen Furgis, and Sophie Saltas presented a report that included survey/questionnaire results from interviews with local parishioners as well as from other Greek communities that operated such facilities. Survey

• An elevator was installed at Holy Trinity Church, thanks to a donation by Theros Sargetis.

• Because of a financial crisis, all parish employee salaries were frozen for the year.

• In November, Archbishop Iakovos presented the St. Paul Award for service to the Salt Lake Greek Orthodox Church and community to Mary Diamant, Pete Gustas, George C. Furgis, Paul Maritsas, James P. Pappas, Constantine J. Skedros.

• Helen Zeese Papanikolas received the Distinguished Alumni Award presented by the University of Utah.

findings were mixed and raised several questions. The concept of a seniors' center died for lack of community support.

July: A float called "Olympics of 1984" was entered in the annual Days of '47 Parade. Under the leadership of sisters Kay Koulis and May Gooras, the float project was supported by donations and by the active participation of the parish youth. The float received the Mayor's Award for the Best Community Float in the parade.

1986

Archbishop Iakovos visited Salt Lake City in March to help commemorate the 80th anniversary of the founding of the city's Greek community, an observance that had been carried over from 1985. A banquet at the Hellenic Memorial Cultural Center on March 1 also attracted Bishop Anthimos of Denver. After an address by the Archbishop, Harry Mark Petrakis, Greek-American author, gave the keynote address. The master of ceremonies was former Utah Governor Scott Matheson.

March 2: Archbishop Iakovos announced the Holy Trinity Church of Salt Lake City would be elevated to the status of a cathedral.

The Archbishop awarded Sam W. Souvall and Paul Borovilos the St. Paul Medal for Service. Honored posthumously with the same award were Maria Takis and Anna Mouskondis who were recognized for organizing the Greek community's first Sunday school in the early 1930s.

Church Friction

The year 1986 was marked by friction related to the concept of two churches under one governing body. Fr. Mahalares, in an effort to divide the workload and responsibilities of the clergy, announced in May that in September he would assign one of his assistants permanently to Prophet Elias Church. Archbishop Iakovos and Bishop Anthimos encouraged this action.

When Fr. Mahalares had arrived in 1981, he stated that he did not approve the concept of the Proistameno (head clergyman) serving one parish with two churches. He believed, as did other former clergy, that it was difficult for clergy to divide their efforts between churches while attempting to become well acquainted with parishioners in both churches.

"In 1950–53, I thought, someone bring me here, so I bring somebody else and maybe he bring somebody else and a lot of people come from Greece…So I bring quite a few of them…I bring a lot— about 15–16…" [The first two were from Crete and attended the University of Utah.]

—*George Adondakis, b. 1902*
Greek Oral History Collection

Parishioners became concerned that such a move would lead to the eventual division of the church-community. On May 19, 1986, the Parish Council, reacting to Fr. Mahalares' suggestion, voted 9 to 4 in favor of the clergy continuing to alternate between churches. The council also endorsed the single-community concept with a single Parish Council that was in place. The issue was temporarily resolved, when Fr. Mahalares, in a letter to the community dated June 2, announced there would be no changes made in clergy assignments.

Later that summer the issue reappeared when a problem developed between Fr. Mahalares and his assistant, Fr. Nick Moskovitis. A group of parishioners from Prophet Elias Church approached Bishop Anthimos requesting that Fr. Moskovitis be assigned permanently to that church. When the Bishop granted the request, Fr. Mahalares became upset and, citing lack of support from the Parish Council, his assistants and his Bishop, he asked for a transfer as soon as possible.

• Also in May 1986, a group of parishioners, determined to perpetuate the Greek culture, language, history, and the Orthodox faith in the region, organized the Hellenic Cultural Association. Its primary purpose was to create a cultural museum that would incorporate the Greek Exhibit, prepared by Helen Zeese Papanikolas and displayed at the State Historical Society Museum. Later, in January 1990, the Parish Council agreed to lease the lower level of Holy Trinity Cathedral to the association for a dollar a year to house a museum. The cultural association assumed all costs related to the site renovation and museum's operation.

November 1986: The Greek community's Thanksgiving dinner for homeless and shut-in individuals was inaugurated. Volunteers served more than 600 guests a traditional Thanksgiving meal. This event now serves more than 3,000 in the Hellenic Memorial Building each year.

1987

March: Sarah Phillips, Nola Slager, and Margo Sotiriou were recognized at the annual Greek Independence Day Banquet for their innovative curriculum developed for the community's Greek-language schools.

March: The Parish Council, in an effort to ban the practice of borrowing from restricted funds—and desirous of repaying earlier debts—presented the following motion to a special general assembly:

> That a Greek Orthodox Church Trust Committee be established to oversee and make certain that special designated and donated funds are used for the express purpose for which they were designated or donated and for no other reason.
>
> That the initial members of the committee shall be Paul Liapis, Tom McGrath, Elyce Mouskondis, Mark Papanikolas, Harry Pappasideris, Margo Sotiriou, the Proistamenos and the President of the Parish Council.

The motion was passed unanimously. The general assemblies of 1987 and 1988 mandated that funds borrowed from designated and donated funds would be replaced with proceeds from Greek Festivals, fund-raising events, and from surplus budget funds as they became available. All such funds were fully replaced within a few years.

July 3, 4, and 5: The 12th annual conference of the Federation of Greek Orthodox Choirs of the Western States attracted some 1,000 choir members, their families, and several clergy. They included: His Grace, Bishop Anthimos of the Denver Diocese, and His Grace, Bishop Anthony of the San Francisco Diocese. Co-chairs for the conference were Sarah Phillips and Yvonne Pauls. Guest conductor was Dr. Theodore Bogdanos, Oakland, California, who was assisted by Paul Maritsas, director of the two Salt Lake choirs.

July 1987: A mission of the Evangelical Antiochian Orthodox Church was established in Salt Lake City under the auspices of Antiochian Archdiocese and in full communion with the Greek Orthodox Archdiocese. However, Parish Council members and some parishioners expressed concern that the new church could adversely impact the established church.

The mission's primary appeal was that the Divine Liturgy was carried out in English. This rekindled the long-simmering issue of whether Greek, English, or both should be used in the liturgy. The mission continued to be a concern among some

sectors of the parish over the next few years as some parishioners joined the newly organized group. However, after a few years, most of these individuals returned to the original church-community.

The Antiochian movement enjoyed moderate growth and, late in the Twentieth Century, it purchased a one-time Jewish synagogue at 355 South 300 East in Salt Lake City. The Sts. Peter & Paul Antiochian Orthodox Church has a very active parish, and it holds services with the full communion of the Greek Orthodox Archdiocese.

The 1994 Thanksgiving dinner for homeless and shut-in individuals was a delicious feast, thanks to this group of volunteers.

1988

April 24: The Hellenic Cultural Association, the Pan Cretan Association of America, the local Pan Cretan Minos Chapter, related Cretan [also known as Pancretan] organizations, and the Greek community acknowledged the significant contributions made by Greek immigrants and those who had served in wars, by dedicating a monument at Holy Trinity in their honor. Inscriptions on the monument pay tribute to:

–*The founding of the Salt Lake Greek community in 1905*

–*The 15 Greek parishioners killed in World War I*

–*The 23 parishioners (including Greek Americans from Price, Utah) killed in World War II*

–*The 49 Greek miners killed in 1924 at a Castle Gate coal mine explosion*

–*150 Greeks who were killed in industrial and mine accidents in Utah between 1904 and 1988*

–*Korean War casualties*

–*The 16 Greek railroad workers killed in 1904 at the Lucin Cutoff.*

June: A committee charged with raising funds for the purchase of a large pipe organ at Holy Trinity Cathedral presented a plan, but no immediate action was taken. Committee members were Nick Cozakos, Wilma Dimas, George Dimas, Ellen Furgis, Diamond Miles, Dorothy Cayias, Nancy Vidalakis, George Miller, and Vida Riddle.

November 20: The pipe organ proposal resurfaced when the persistent committee presented another plan to the general assembly. This plan carried a total cost of $168,000, with $13,000 earmarked for renovating the balcony; $25,000 for a perpetual organ fund, and $130,000 to purchase and install the organ. Further, the committee emphasized it would be responsible for raising all funds. After a prolonged debate, the assembly voted down the proposal, 30–27, based on fear that the interior of the church would be extensively altered.

The following March (1989), George Dimas, speaking on behalf of the committee, reported that the cathedral organ would be purchased with donations, including some from out of state, and that the committee had received a $20,000 donation, plus other lesser gifts. After a heated debate and a secret ballot vote, the organ plan was defeated, 97–50.

Fr. Joachim Hatzidakis conducted Memorial Day services, May 27, 1990.

1989

January: Mario Giannopoulos was appointed as the parish's full-time youth director and Basil Chelemes was named athletic director. Both positions were vital in terms of developing youth activities for the community.

March: Agreement was reached on the purchase of the so-called "7–11 property" located north of Holy Trinity/ Hellenic Memorial Building on the corner of 200 South and 300 West. The price was $370,000. A donation of $104,000 from Diamond Miles and proceeds from Greek Festival 1989 accelerated the purchase process.

June: In an effort to assist in the relocation to Salt Lake City of several Russian immigrant families, the Parish Council offered them two-year free memberships to the parish. Fr. Ioachim Hatzidakis appealed to the community to donate clothing, and the Slavic-American Cultural Society and the Greek community sponsored an evening of Russian culture to raise funds.

August 15: The International Greek Folklore Society (Laographia) from Southern California, the Hellenic Cultural Association of Salt Lake City and the Cretans of Utah presented a series of cultural activities at Prophet Elias Church and at Park City, Utah. The purpose of this Greek Folklore Symposium was to develop an appreciation and understanding of Greek music, dance, folklore, and musical instruments. It attracted participants and attendees from various parts of the United States and Greece, many of them experts. One of the highlights of the gathering was the performance by "GRIGKILOS," a dance group from Chania, Crete, at the International Dance Festival in Spanish Fork, Utah. The Folklore Society was under the direction of Kathy Politopoulos.

• The financial, political, and spiritual challenges presented to the Greek Orthodox community by the decade of the 1980s had caused strong reactions within the Parish. Passions ran high as fervor for individual and group goals arose in conflict. To the credit of the church-community as a devoted body, their cultural offerings educated the Greater Salt Lake community and focused their faithful efforts toward a future that would have made their immigrant forebears proud.

"…we'd leave Bingham and come down (to Salt Lake) to church. That's 30 miles from here…But always, someone here would invite the out-of-towners to their home to eat—but the out-of-towners always brought something with them to supplement what was on the other man's table…usually they'd always bring a jug of wine. Or bread. And olives and cheese, whatever."

—*John Chipian, b. 1923*
Greek Oral History Collection

Archbishop Iakovos conducted the consecration of Prophet Elias Church in July 1991, assisted by Bishop Isaiah.

Chapter 8

Consecration of Prophet Elias Church

The Twentieth Century's last decade began on a note of celebration. Combining traditions of the mother country with a desire to share their Greek heritage, Greek-American parishioners of the several Orthodox churches throughout the Intermountain West often joined forces on sacred, social, and celebratory occasions.

Pantokrator at Prophet Elias Church.

Greek Independence Day commemoration festivities and the 85th anniversary celebration of the Salt Lake church-community held in 1990 were among the celebration highlights. Expansion, improvements, and vision portended great things for the coming Twenty-first Century.

1990

March: At the Greek Independence Day celebration, John Chipian and Ellen Furgis were honored by the Utah Arts Council. It was announced at the banquet that the Ethnic Minority Archives of the Oral History Institute of Utah had been moved to the J. Willard Marriott Library at the University of Utah. Some Greek archives were included in the ethnic material. A contribution of $10,000 by the Greek community made this move possible.

July: Syd Colessides presented a plan prepared by Douglas Anderson to landscape the courtyard between the Holy Trinity Cathedral and the cultural center. She told the council she would raise $25,000 to complete the project. The plan was approved and the landscaping was completed in the summer of 1992.

October: The church-community celebrated its 85th anniversary with a banquet at the Marriott Hotel where Bishop Isaiah was principal speaker. He presented awards for service and contributions to the church-community to Diamond Miles, Kay Floor, and Constantine J. Skedros. George C. Furgis, Estelle Kevitch, Kaliopi Sargetakis, and Nick Colessides directed anniversary activities.

Anniversary activities included a musical play, "What a Day," presented by community thespians in November. It was written and directed by Paul Maritsas and Nicole Pauls. Cast members were Basil Anton, Gregory Anastasopoulos, Nick Colessides, Andy Giannis, George Karahalios, Bus Lazarakis, Liz Mallas, Sophie Mallas, Vassi Maritsas, George Miller, and Anna and Valerie Wondolowski.

Greek-American Senator Elected

In November of 1990, parishioner George E. Mantes (D), a Tooele auto dealership owner, was elected to the Utah State Senate representing Tooele and Juab counties. In November 1994, he was re-elected to his Senate post and later served on the Utah State Board of Regents.

Consecration of Prophet Elias

The consecration of Prophet Elias Church on July 21 was the most memorable event of 1991. More than 1,000 attended, with many watching the services in the church hall on closed-circuit television. Archbishop Iakovos conducted the sacred service that included sealing the relics of St. Haralambos and St. Boniface under the altar.

Among bishops and clergy participating with Archbishop Iakovos were:

Bishop Isaiah, Chancellor, Greek Orthodox Archdiocese

The Rev. Joachim Hatzidakis, Proistamenos,
  Holy Trinity Cathedral and Prophet Elias Church

The Rev. John Kaloudis, assistant priest, Holy Trinity Cathedral
  and Prophet Elias Church

The Rev. George Politis, assistant priest, Holy Trinity Cathedral
  and Prophet Elias Church

The Rev. Constantine Palassis, retired

Deacon Anatoli Kereiev, Deacon, Holy Trinity Cathedral
  and Prophet Elias Church.

A musical program by the combined choirs of Holy Trinity Cathedral and Prophet Elias Church had honored Archbishop Iakovos on the previous Friday. A banquet at Little America Hotel the next day attracted 625 people. An open house and the annual church-community picnic at Prophet Elias added to the festivities.

Visiting Clergy:

The Rev. Milton Gianoulis, St. Andrews Greek Orthodox
Church, Chicago (he served in Salt Lake City in the 1980s)

The Rev. Makarios Mannos, St. Nicholas Greek Orthodox
Church, Grand Junction, Colorado (a native of
Salt Lake City)

The Rev. Angelo Michaels, Transfiguration Greek Orthodox
Church, Ogden

The Rev. Luke G. Kontgas, Transfiguration Greek Orthodox
Church, Anchorage, Alaska (native of Price, Utah)

The Rev. Elias Stephanopoulos, Holy Trinity Greek Orthodox
Church, Portland, Oregon (first priest to serve at Prophet
Elias Church in 1969)

The Rev. Kallinikos Petsas, Assumption Greek Orthodox
Church, Price

The Rev. Joseph Strezelki, Prophet Elias Greek
Orthodox Church, Santa Cruz, California (a native of Salt
Lake City)

The Rev. John Travis, Transfiguration Greek Orthodox Church,
Austin, Texas

Deacon Peter Alex, Transfiguration Greek Orthodox Church,
Ogden, (a native of Layton, Utah)

1991

April: The Denver Diocese Clergy-Laity Conference in
Salt Lake City attracted numerous clergy and laity delegates,
including Rev. Nick Triantofilou, Vicar General, Greek
Orthodox Archdiocese from New York City, and Dena
Skouras Oldknow, Los Angeles, national president of the
Philoptochos Society.

Prophet Elias Consecration Committee, 1991: Co-Chairman Ted J. Speros, front row left, William Kandas, Mary K. Diamant, The Very Reverend Joachim Hatzidakis, General Chairman Chris S. Metos, Mary R. Musuris, Diana M. Fowler, Dean Athens, John A. Chipian, Paul D. Maritsas; Bill Thomas Peters, top row left, Lefty Landures, Andy Katsanevas, Sam Chelemes, Basil S. Chelemes, Peter W. G. Cayias, and Stanley M. Kouris.

June: The University of Utah College of Humanities, and the language and literature departments, awarded parishioner William D. Cocorinis an outstanding teaching award for his work in the Modern Greek-language program.

October: The community celebrated paying off the mortgage on the La France Apartments during a luncheon in the Hellenic Cultural Center. The celebration was particularly significant because, for the first time in years, the community was debt-free.

1992

Cultural Museum Dedicated

May 3: The community realized a long-discussed dream when the Hellenic Cultural Museum was dedicated at Holy Trinity Cathedral. The museum, located on the lower level of the Holy Trinity Cathedral is the first Greek ethnic museum in the United States, and represents more than $100,000 in donations and in-kind services. The primary emphasis of its collection is on Greek history (classical and modern), Eastern Orthodoxy, comparative religions, and Greek-American history. The idea for the museum dated to May 23, 1986, with the establishment of the Hellenic Cultural Association, under the stewardship of Chris Metos. The origin of the museum began with the concept of creating a repository of old photographs of Greek-immigrant activities in Utah. In the early 1980s, a small group of native- born Greek Americans started collecting and identifying old photographs. The collection has become a repository for archival materials and is operated by a paid part-time librarian and a host of volunteers. Included are various artifacts, oral history interviews, and videos of immigrant and family activities.

Goal of the association was to establish a museum "to preserve the rich history, heritage, and traditions that reflect the Greek experience in the Intermountain West, particularly in Utah." Toward that goal, numerous parish families donated memorabilia to the museum. The association also was anxious to find a permanent home for "The Greek Exhibit" which had been on display at the Utah State Historical Society Museum during 1982–1984.

The museum is a "People's Museum." Since its opening in May 1992, approximately 55,000 individuals of all ages have visited the exhibit. It has become a major attraction during the annual Greek Festival. The museum is open on Wednesday mornings and Sunday afternoons after church services. Tours can be scheduled in advance during the week. There is no admission fee.

The museum activities have been supported by a dedicated group of volunteer parishioners who have given thousands of hours of service. Among these are Andy Katsanevas, Bill and Sophie Drossos, Thano Castles, John Chipian, Louis Thiros, Bill Rekouniotis, Jim Kastanis, and Constantine J. Skedros.

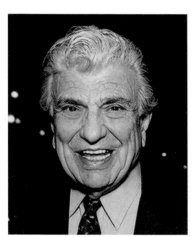

William D. Cocorinis, longtime University of Utah teacher.

A small gift shop, located within the museum, offers a good collection of books by Greek-American authors. In addition, a variety of cultural and religious items from Greece can be purchased. Since 1992, both the museum and the library have been operating with volunteers, though professional help was used to implement the grant from the Burton Foundation.

The museum was honored in 1992 when it was the recipient of the Utah Heritage Award given by the Utah Heritage Foundation. In 1994, it received a certificate of commendation from the American Association of State and Local History. It was the only ethnic museum honored that year. On January 18, 1996, during Utah's Statehood Centennial celebration, the Utah House and State Senate passed a commemorative resolution honoring the Hellenic Cultural Museum.

Other 1992 Highlights

March: Diamond Miles donated $69,000 to remodel the dining room and kitchen facilities at the Hellenic Memorial Cultural Center. Over the years, Mrs. Miles has been a major benefactor, contributing between $1.5-2 million.

May 17: Youth Appreciation Night honored the community's Greek dance groups, Greek Orthodox Youth of America (GOYA), and high school graduates. Awards were presented to Alethia Bapis, Briana Koucos, Michael Bapis,

Banners and photos of Greek-American groups are among items displayed at the Hellenic Cultural Museum.

Zachary Koucos, Bobby Benson, Kristi Landures, Briana Benson, Bus Lazarakis, Jason Cowan, Jason McGrath, Gregory Floor, Jason Mihalopoulos, Mike Johnson, Jonathan Pappasideris, Jami Karahalios, Angela Parenti, Christina Kartsonis, Michael Parenti, Michael Katsanevas, Tom Peters, Lexie Katsanevas, T. J. Speros, Katheryn Kireiev, Tony Varanakis, and Tatiana Kireiev. Also honored was Diana M. Fowler, the parish's youth director.

Annual Greek Festival

The highly successful Greek Festival was recognized in 1992. Salt Lake City's Downtown Alliance presented to the Greek Orthodox community an award for staging the annual event.

Greek Festival dance performances draw a standing-room-only crowd. This Junior GOYA Dance Group entertained Festival-goers in 1996.

Pastries are a festival favorite of visitors as are other flavorful Greek food selections. Festival goers also browse at shops that sell icons, clothing from Greece, foodstuffs, and T-shirts touting the festival-related 5K run. Cooking demonstrations and a children's midway are other popular attractions.

Staged under large temporary tents in the Holy Trinity Cathedral parking area and in the adjacent Hellenic Memorial Building, the festival also features tours of the Hellenic Association Museum and the cathedral where the choir offers performances. The festival has grown to foster camaraderie and volunteerism among parishioners of all ages who serve as greeters and who prepare and serve food, work as cashiers, and set-up and maintain facilities.

The energetic performances by the community's talented youth dance groups and the Dionysus Dancers who perform authentic dancing in traditional costumes are often crowd favorites.

Scope of the festival was expanded in 1987 when a marathon was added that evolved into the Greek Classic that includes a 5-K health walk, 5-K race, and 10-K race. Held annually on the first day of the festival, the classic attracts some 1,500 entrants, including some who participate on roller-blades and those who compete in children's and handicapped/wheelchair divisions. The Greek Classic and the Greek Festival are prominently promoted on colorful banners hung on light poles throughout the downtown

Started in 1975 under the chairmanship of Gregory and Jenny Skedros, the festival has been a major showcase for the Salt Lake Greek community while raising funds for area charities as well as church-related projects and programs. Held the weekend after Labor Day in September, it is a three-day celebration of Greek culture, traditions, history, religion, and exceptional food offerings. It has become the region's largest ethnic festival, attracting some 40,000, including civic, business, and political leaders, many of whom volunteer as servers.

district and are well publicized by area print media and on radio and television.

August 1992: Stephanie Chachas was hired as full-time parish youth director. This came at a time when the community was particularly concerned about the increasing needs of its youth and its numerous youth-related activities. Previously, youth directors worked on a volunteer basis or on a part-time assignment from other parish positions. Volunteers to youth programs have included, among many others, the following: Andy Takis, Jr., Deedee Tikoff, Mary M. Thiros, Mario Giannopoulos, Basil S. Chelemes, Nick Bapis, George Varanakis, Gus Teseros, Bob Babalis, John Calevas, Diana M. Fowler, and Michael Daskalas.

November 22: Holy Trinity Cathedral was the site for the annual Community Service of Thanksgiving, sponsored by the local chapter of the National Conference of Christians and Jews (now called the National Conference of Community and Justice). Principal speaker was Arthur K. Smith, president of the University of Utah. The choirs of Holy Trinity Cathedral and Prophet Elias Church provided music for the event. Members of the community affiliated with the local chapter of the NCCJ have included Ted J. Speros, Bill Thomas Peters, Nick S. Vidalakis, Constantine J. Skedros, Ted Sargetakis, and Myrlene Korologos, who served as the organization's executive director for17 years.

1993

Records show the Parish Council priorities for the church and community in February 1993 were: "Faith in God," "A United Community," "Education in Our Faith," "Meeting the Needs of the Parishioners," and "Liturgical Participation." The priorities were not new—they have been the basic ingredients that have nurtured the growth of the Greek Orthodox community of Salt Lake City since 1905.

Mary Adondakis, left, Mary Barnes, Pat Takas; Stella Saltas, back left, Nola Slager, Effie Kosta, Margo Sotiriou, Anna Makris, Stella Papanikolas, Demetra Thimakis, Diane Johnson, Louis Thiros, and Ellen Furgis prepared pans of baklava for a Greek Festival.

Greek Independence Day observances have always featured children from the Greek school classes. These young performers recited poems and sang during a 1980's event.

March: The community's Greek Independence Day observance continued its tradition of honoring Greek school teachers. Elaine Bovos, Angie Bournakis, Tony Mae Dwyer, Venus Koukouvetakis, Cathy Neofitos, and Zeta Tsagaris were recognized.

1994

July: Greece's ambassador to the United States, Lucas Tsilas, joined Fr. John Kaloudis and William D. Cocorinis in a meeting with the General Authorities of the Church of Jesus Christ of Latter-day Saints (LDS-Mormon) in which the activities of the Mormon missionaries in Greece were discussed. The ambassador said he had been instructed by the Greek government to convey to the LDS Church leadership his government's concern regarding membership-proselytizing activities by LDS missionaries in Greece. He informed the LDS Church leaders that the constitution of Greece forbids non-orthodox groups from proselytizing in Greece.

Prophet Elias Multi-purpose Center

In November 1994, the general assembly, after a lengthy discussion, approved the construction of a gymnasium at Prophet Elias Church.

Subsequently, the project changed in scope from building a gymnasium to building a multi-purpose center, including St. Sophia School.

For several years the Hellenic Memorial Building had served the athletic, educational, and cultural needs of the church-community. Construction of a gymnasium at Prophet Elias Church became a significant topic among parishioners in 1994, although it had been discussed formally since 1977 when the parish's Planning and Development Committee recommended one be built at the site within the next 15 years.

A motion, passed at the November 20, 1994, general assembly, approved "the spending of the necessary funds in order to construct the building shell, infrastructure, and architectural engineering up to $531,970." The motion also "authorized the board to borrow the required funds, subject to raising a minimum of $150,000 prior to construction."

A petition signed by 117 parishioners in January slowed the process. It called for a special general assembly to be held February 25, 1995. At that meeting numerous items pertaining to the project were discussed—again. The assembly approved the project as proposed in the 1994 general assembly by a vote of 135–76.

The fund-raising committee raised more than $1.3 million. In 1998 additional funds were raised by the sale of commemorative bricks that each cost $1,200. Unfortunately, only 15 to 20 percent of parishioners bought such a brick.

Parish Councils between 1995 and 1998 saw unanticipated expenses add to the cost of the project. These included costs of replacing existing Sunday school rooms, providing facilities for an Orthodox school, constructing a new and larger kitchen, and escalating building costs. General assembly records show the proposal on November 24, 1994, carried a price tag of $531,970; on February 26, 1995, it was $918.580; on April 26, 1996, it was $1.23 million, and by November 23, 1997, it had reached $2.17 million.

Through the efforts of the Hellenic Heritage Campaign and rental income realized during the Olympic Winter Games of 2002, the Prophet Elias Multi-purpose Center became debt-free. Prime movers for the construction of the multi-purpose center were Parish Council members and Nick Bapis, Douglas Anderson, (whose Union Pointe Construction Company waived a $168,000 contractor's fee), Peter W. G. Cayias, and David Katsanevas.

1995

The biennial national conference of the Young Adult League of the Greek Orthodox Archdiocese (Y.A.L.) was held June 30-July 5 at Utah's Snowbird Ski and Summer Resort. This was the first time this meeting was held outside a major metropolitan area. It attracted more than 900 young adults and several clergy, including Bishop Kallistos from England, who gave the keynote address, and Bishop Isaiah from the Denver Diocese.

The steering committee for the conference consisted of Mark and Stacy Kouris and George and Kim Adondakis, Fr. John Kaloudis, Fr. Dean Panagos, Nicole Pauls, Pam Zoumadakis, Sophie Mallas, Pete Giamalakis, Elenie G. Sefandonakis, Mary Zervos, Dean Athens, Bus Lazarakis, Angela Peters, Cindy Skedros, Georgene Colovos, Patricia Pippas, Jorge Daskalakis, Lisa Kalantzes, John Giannopoulos, Andrea Pullos, Ted Sargetakis, Ted Paulos, Angel Skedros, Perry Drossos, and Rita Papadakis.

October: The parish observed its 90th anniversary with several activities:

> –A musical play, dedicated to the early Greek arrivals to Utah, was directed and produced by Paul Maritsas
>
> –A lecture, "The Future of Orthodoxy in America," by James C. Skedros, Th.D., associate professor of church history at the Greek Orthodox School of Theology, Brookline, Massachusetts

Greek Festival, 1996.

Chris S. Metos, President, Hellenic Cultural Association, 1986–2004.

–A doxology at Holy Trinity Cathedral commemorating
the events of 1905, the year the local Greek Orthodox
Church was founded

–The anniversary banquet attracted more than 675,
including representatives of the Ecumenical Patriarch
Bartholomew from Constantinople (Istanbul), and
several other local, regional, and national clerics

–Archbishop Stylianos and Bishop Isaiah, upon the
authority of Ecumenical Patariarch, conferred on
Constantine J. Skedros the title of Archon Deputos of
the Great Church. Other parishioners who have been
awarded Archon status in the Greek Orthodox
Community of Salt Lake City include John Billinis,
Nicholas L. Strike, John L. Strike, George L. Strike,
Tom C. Korologos, Peter W. G. Cayias, and
Nick S. Vidalakis.

1996

February: Hellenic Cultural Association officers Chris S.
Metos, Bill Drossos, and Constantine J. Skedros asked the
Parish Council for a long-term lease for space to house the
Strike Library, named in memory of its benefactor, Louis N.
Strike, Salt Lake businessman and church leader who died
in 1967. The association said it would operate the library
in the Hellenic Memorial Building and develop it into a
research center on Hellenism and Orthodoxy to serve the

Intermountain West. The council unanimously approved
the lease request.

Other 1996 Highlights

The Salt Lake City Housing Authority demanded certain
items be rectified immediately at the La France Apartments.
The general assembly agreed to raze the La France garages,
located east of the apartments. This was accomplished in
January 1997, facilitating a parking lot.

December: The parish learned construction costs for the
Prophet Elias Multi-purpose Center had increased from $1.2
million to $1.8 million, due primarily to the addition of an
educational wing.

• The general assembly allocated $38,000 for a feasibility
study on the need for further renovation of Holy Trinity
Cathedral. The study, prepared by TBA Architects and Culp
Construction, indicated it would cost $4.2 million for a
seismic upgrade of the venerable structure.

1997

May: The community's historical offerings were greatly
enhanced with the opening of the Hellenic Cultural
Association/Strike Library in the Hellenic Memorial Building.
The library immediately became the repository of more than
1,000 Greek and English historical and religious volumes,
including newspapers and magazines. Later, in 2000, a $25,000

Youth retreat with Fr. Joachim Hatzidakis, 1992.

grant from the R. Harold Burton Foundation funded the purchase of a computer and software that allowed museum volunteers to catalogue hundreds of books and artifacts as well as to digitize more than 1,000 photographs. Like the Hellenic Cultural Museum, the library was initiated by, and is under the auspices of, the Hellenic Cultural Association and is operated by paid part-time librarians and a host of volunteers who maintain its archives on Greek history (classical and modern), Eastern Orthodoxy, comparative religions, and Greek-American history.

Renovation of Holy Trinity Cathedral
During 1997, the renovation of the Holy Trinity dome and roof was underway. This was the first phase of the restoration of the Cathedral.

Culp Construction was given the contract. The project was completed in 1998.

Funds for this project had been allocated from previous festivals. The estimated cost was between $450,000 and $500,000. Working with the contractors was the Church Building Committee: Sam Chelemes, Andy Hatupis, Andy Katsanevas, Bill Rekouniotis, George Miller, Bill Kandas, and Tony Thimakis. This committee, through the years has given valuable service to the community.

• In June, Tony Thimakis, a native of Salt Lake City, was named executive director of the church-community on the retirement of Bill Kandas, who had held the post since 1978.

Proud oratorical contest winners show off their awards in Salt Lake City in June 1996 with Bishop Isaiah. The competition is held annually by the Greek Orthodox Archdiocese of North and South America.

Saint Sophia Hellenic Orthodox School

Opened in 1997 with a pre-school and kindergarten, the Hellenic Orthodox School on the grounds of Prophet Elias Church, was given the name of St. Sophia Hellenic Orthodox School in 1998. Sarah Phillips, a former public school teacher, was its first principal. She had served as a member of the Holy Trinity Cathedral Choir.

After remarkable progress, elementary grades one through six were added and within a few years the school became financially independent from the Parish Council, thanks to successful fund-raising efforts.

First graduating class of St. Sophia School on May 26, 2004 consisted of, front, from left: Aaron Gilbert, Dimitri Litsas, Vincent Meyer, Paul Chaus and principal Patricia Pignanelli. Back, from left, Nyman Brooks instructor; Justin Tilley, Pilar Pappas, Katina Pappadakis, Mathew Chaus.

The founders of St. Sophia Hellenic Orthodox School, Elaine M. Bapis, left, Margo Sotiriou, and Vickie Folias, received the Medal of St. Paul in 2004.

The school of nearly 100 students held its first graduation for sixth-grade students May 26, 2004. The school's first graduates were Matthew Chaus, Paul Chaus, Aaron Gilbert, Demetrios Litsas, Vincent Meyer, Katina Papadakis, Pilar Pappas, and Justin Tilley. During these ceremonies, the school's founders: Margo Sotiriou, Vickie Folias, and Elaine Bapis—all of Salt Lake City—received the Medal of Saint Paul through the recommendation of Metropolitan Isaiah of Denver and with the blessing of Archbishop Demetrios of America.

St. Sophia School is the only one of its kind in Utah to teach Modern Greek. In addition to the core curriculum, students attend church and religion classes, have access to a library, computer lab, and participate in an enriched physical education program.

An editorial in the *Salt Lake Tribune*, on February 15, 1998, lauded the efforts of the parish in establishing the school.

New School Adds Diversity

St. Sophia Hellenic Orthodox School is a new, worthwhile educational alternative in the Salt Lake Valley and further evidence of the growing cultural maturity and educational diversity of many Utahns.

The year-old school is still small, offering preschool through first grade to 33 students. Next fall, a second grade will be added.

Like parochial schools operated by Roman Catholics, Lutherans and others in the Salt Lake area, St. Sophia offers academic instruction as well as teaching about the faith— specifically that of the Greek Orthodox Church.

Because Eastern Orthodox Christianity historically has taken specific cultural and ethnic lines (Greek, Russian, Serbian, Antiochian, etc.) while retaining doctrinal purity, part of religious education at St. Sophia involves Greek culture and its larger Hellenic manifestations.

This alone likely will give St. Sophia's students an edge over their peers when it comes to historical knowledge. Hellenic culture, history and civilization are not much emphasized in Utah's public schools, although these things have affected and continued to affect human civilization.

The new school fills a natural and obvious niche in the growing community. Salt Lake's Greek Orthodox parish is a well-established, integral part of the community. For years, it has been interested in education, offering Greek language classes as well as religious instruction to parishioners.

The recent decision of a group of parishioners to start a parochial school was a logical one that apparently addresses a community need. It is no accident that Salt Lake's Greek Orthodox parish itself decided to provide facilities for the fledgling school.

Utah's capital is becoming a more mature, diverse and sophisticated place. The growing variety of educational alternatives—parochial and secular—both reflects and adds to this fact. In this spirit, St. Sophia's is a welcome addition to the community's educational diversity.

—*Salt Lake Tribune*
February 15, 1998

Final Year of Twentieth Century, 1999

The last year of the Twentieth Century began with a renewed focus on the restoration of Holy Trinity Cathedral, a project that had strong support but was opposed by a number of council members.

January 25: The proposed fund-raising program presented by Fund Raising Consultants Inc. (FRCI), the group working with the Cathedral Restoration Committee, was the subject of spirited discussion. Most Parish Council members agreed that between $6 million and $8 million could be raised in the community, but it was apparent that many council members opposed the Cathedral Square Project.

A study made by parishioner Tom Peterson showed that 32 percent of parishioners lived north of 2100 South and 68 percent lived south of 2100 South. The council decided to initiate a series of open discussions, beginning in March, to find out what parishioners thought of the project and how much they would support it.

February 6: The Parish Council visited the Hellenic Memorial Cultural Center to examine its physical condition in an effort to determine whether remodeling or new construction was the prudent action. The council was told that FRCI believed that a minimum lead gift of $5 million would make it possible to raise as much as $16 million more for the restoration project.

• In March, the annual Greek Independence Day banquet was highlighted by the announcement that Ted J. Speros had created a $100,000 endowment fund for the community.

June 27: A special general assembly concerning the proposed Cathedral restoration and related projects included a discussion regarding a presentation by Douglas Anderson and Nick Bapis. Anderson made the following motion that was seconded by David Katsanevas:

> *Resolved: That the Special General Assembly supports the fund-raising efforts with a focus on the Holy Trinity Cathedral plus Sunday School classrooms, administration, dining hall, cultural center, and Museum as recommended by the fund-raising committee and approved by the General Assembly.*

The motion passed by a vote of 76 to 1 with 2 abstentions. The apathy of the community was evident in the attendance. With a membership of more than 1,000, only 75 attended—less than 8 percent of parish members.

• As a result of a computer problem in the church office, the new directory was not printed on time. A donation of $18,000 by Nick Bapis and Gus and Tommie Sotiriou allowed the purchase of a new computer system, which was installed, at no cost to the community, by parishioner Ron Ferguson.

August 23: The Parish Council was informed of a letter from Metropolitan Isaiah, concerning the recent tornado in Salt Lake City whose destructive force had missed Holy Trinity Cathedral by one block. He criticized the community for planning to spend millions of dollars to restore the Cathedral. In June, the council had discussed a request for $250,000 from the Metropolitan for the proposed Diocese Center in Denver. Council members objected to the request since the Salt Lake community was raising funds for the Cathedral restoration.

In his August letter, the Metropolitan also recommended Fr. Mathew Gilbert, from Price, as a replacement for Fr. Tsaras who had gone to Oklahoma City in June.

• Fr. Kaloudis told the council that Deacon Louie Koucos wished to be ordained to the priesthood and that although the Metropolitan had given his official blessing, final Archdiocese approval had not yet been received. Deacon Koucos, who had been assisting the clergy in various liturgical activities, had indicated that he was willing to attend a program at Holy Cross School of Theology in Brookline, Massachusetts.

September 14: The Parish Council voted to accept Fr. Gilbert, who had expressed a special interest in the youth groups, and also approved the hiring of Deacon Koucos as part-time financial manager and as part-time youth director. Late in 1999, upon the resignation of Tony Thimakis as executive director, Deacon Koucos was appointed temporary executive director and financial manager.

- The promise of a new millennium's opportunities for Church-community growth saw 1999 close on an uplifting note with plans for expansion, renovation, and celebration in the Twenty-first Century.

Clergy: 1972–2002

The Rev. George Politis, 1972–present
The Rev. Stratten Dorozenski, 1972–1974
The Rev. John Papaionaides, 1975–1977
The Rev. Dean Gigicos, 1975–1981
The Rev. Milton Gianoulis, 1980–1982
The Rev. Andrew Mahalares, 1981–1987
The Rev. Emanuel Lillios, 1982–1984
The Rev. Nicholas Moskovitis, 1984–1987
The Rev. Joachim Hatzidakis 1987–1991
The Rev. John Kaloudis, 1987–2002

Fr. John Kaloudis, conducted this service in Holy Trinity Cathedral in the 1990s. He had the longest tenure of clergymen serving in Salt Lake City, having served both Greek Orthodox churches from 1987–2002.

"I had the privilege of associating with my grandfather...I'm one of the few people who had a grandfather (in America)."

—John Chipian, b. 1923
Greek Oral History Collection

Prophet Elias Church, 5335 South Highland Drive, Holladay, Utah. Set against the Wasatch Mountains, the church's architecture makes a stunning statement that blends classical column and dome elements with contemporary simplicity.

Chapter 9

Church-Community Solidarity

The new century afforded the parish favorable public exposure and saw the advancement of plans for expanding its cultural facilities. Awareness of the Greek church-community by the Intermountain region's general population continued to grow. Participation in Greek-sponsored activities in the year 2000 and beyond were enthusiastically attended.

Publicity of Greek individuals and groups was achieved with national and international prominence.

Such events as the 2002 Olympic and Paralympic Winter Games, the inaugural of Governor Jon Huntsman Jr., and public television programming were hallmarks of the period. The faith and fervor of Greeks gained wide-ranging respect to a degree early Greek immigrants would have found unimaginable in 1905.

2000

January: The *Salt Lake Tribune* listed its selection of the Top 20 Most Influential Utahns of the Twentieth Century.

The auspicious list included Helen Zeese Papanikolas, with this comment:

> *Helen Papanikolas was a faithful recorder of Utah's rich ethnic heritage whose historical works made it impossible to ignore the complexities of Utah's past and present. Her previous honors included a distinguished alumni award and an honorary doctorate from the University of Utah.*

May 7: The Hellenic Cultural Association, at its annual Founders' Day program, honored Helen Zeese Papanikolas, author and historian, and Kay Koulis, for her many years of community and civic service.

Helen Zeese Papanikolas was selected as an "Influential Utahn" in 2000.

August 19: The $8 million Hellenic Heritage Campaign was launched in August to raise funds for seismic upgrade and other work on Holy Trinity Cathedral, for a proposed cultural campus there, and for debt payoff on the multi-purpose center at Prophet Elias. The event featured remarks by Fr. Kaloudis, John W. Gallivan (publisher emeritus of the *Salt Lake Tribune* and prime mover of the restoration project of Cathedral of the Madeleine), as well as Nick Bapis, Mike C. Korologos, and Constantine J. Skedros. It was announced at this gathering that $2.2 million had been pledged.

November 18: The community's 95th anniversary celebration and banquet on November 18 at the Marriott Hotel was attended by 635 people. Archbishop Demetrios gave the keynote address. Metropolitan Isaiah also attended the function, which was under the general chairmanship of Charlie Cayias.

November 19: The Holladay Community's first annual Inter-faith Thanksgiving Program drew 600 participants on November 19, 2000. Church historian Constantine J. Skedros spoke on the "American Dream—the Story of the Greek Immigrants to Utah and Salt Lake City from 1900."

November: A video documentary, "Utah's Greek Americans," aired on KUED Channel 7, the University of Utah's public television station. Featuring numerous interviews with first- and second-generation Greek-Americans, historic photos, and anecdotes, the program was a favorable public

KUED Channel 7 video documentary, "Utah's Greek Americans," aired in November 2000.

relations vehicle for the parish. The film project originated in November 1999 when the Hellenic Cultural Association was asked by KUED to provide historical background and financial assistance for its production. Toward that end, some $56,000 in financial support came from the Hellenic Cultural Association, the Helen Metos Memorial Fund, the Anna K. Skedros Memorial Fund, Chris and George Metos, the R. Harold Burton Foundation, the Michaels Foundation, Helen Zeese Papanikolas, Bill and Elyce Mouskondis, and Silver State Suppliers.

2001

Honoring significant donors and reaffirmation of solidarity among parishioners of Salt Lake City's two Greek Orthodox Churches highlighted parish activities of the year 2001.

February: The University of Utah Crimson Club, a sports-booster organization, inducted parishioner and baseball player George (The "Stork") Theodore into its hall of fame. He was a former football and basketball player for the university and later played professional baseball for the New York Mets.

March 22: Sixty donors to the Hellenic Heritage Campaign fund drive were honored for their generosity and each received a holy icon and commemorative pin at a reception. During the ceremonies, it was announced that the largest single donation to the church-community—$1.1 million—was presented by the children of the late Christ and Helen Pappasotiriou (Sotiriou): Gus, Tommie, Margo, and Leo Sotiriou and their families. The Salt Lake City-based Eccles Foundation donated $750,000 to the campaign.

May: Salt Lake City's Westminster College staged an alumni activity entitled the "Spirit of Greece." Its honorary committee consisted of William C. and Bonnie Athas, Basil Chelemes, Sylvia Dewey, P. Nick Floros, George and Ellen Furgis, Karen Furgis, Utah State Senator George and Mary Ann Mantes,

Peter and Nicole Mouskondis, Bill and Elyce Mouskondis, and chairpersons Katherine Ellis and Lisa Kalantzes.

May 27: The annual Hellenic Cultural Association Memorial Day Program featured an address by former Salt Lake resident James P. Pappas, Ph.D., vice president of the University of Oklahoma. Receiving special honors at the event were Steve J. Poulos, World War II veteran and Purple Heart recipient, and the late John B. Sergakis, also a war veteran. Others recognized were parishioners who served in the armed forces of Greece from 1940–1950: Theos K. Angelos, George Armaou, Frank Comarell, Nick Corbett. Gus Daskalakis, Pan Doudaniotis, Basil Floor, Peter Gamvroulas, George Gianoulis, James S. Karras, Andrew Katsohirakis, Emanuel Mylonakis, Chris Tsoufakis, Steve Tzerenakis, and the late John Pananos and Gregory Panouses.

As the largest donors to the Capital Campaign, Sotiriou family members took control of symbolic jackhammers at the groundbreaking for the $2.5 million restoration at Holy Trinity Cathedral on July 11, 2004. Participants were Alexander, left, Elysia, Stephen, Leo, Tommie, Chris, Margo, and Antoinette as Fr. Michael Kouremetis, left, and Fr. Matthew Gilbert looked on.

• A meeting of the Greek Orthodox Leadership 100 heard remarks from Fr. Alexander Karloutsos, New York, and Nick S. Vidalakis, who stated the group's goal was to raise funds and provide financial support to the various ministries of the Archdiocese. Parishioners Douglas Anderson and Nick Bapis were inducted as members during the meeting.

October 22: The Parish Council approved the following motion: "…That the by-laws set by the Diocese are adhered to with the exception being that if there is conflict with our parish by-laws, the local guidelines will supersede the Diocese."

The council also voted on the issue of dividing the church-community. The vote was based on whether or not the parish was to adhere to parish bylaws of 1974, which state:

1. *It is an aim of this parish to remain united as one parish, regardless of churches or of property owned;*
2. *The parish shall be known as the Greek Orthodox Church of Greater Salt Lake City.*

All 14 Parish Council members voted to remain united. Five of the 14 emphasized that both churches should be treated equally.

Community Welcomes Olympic Games Visitors

2002

As the host city, Salt Lake City welcomed the world to the Utah capital for the Olympic and Paralympic Winter Games of 2002. The games attracted more than one million visitors, making it the biggest undertaking in the city's history. The local Greek community was well represented and involved in the Games on several fronts.

February 7: The Olympic and Paralympic Winter Games attracted a large delegation of Olympic, cultural and government officials from Greece, many of whom attended a parish-sponsored reception at the Hellenic Memorial Cultural Center. Among the dignitaries attending were Greek Foreign Minister George Papandreou; Cultural Minister Evangelos Venizelos; chairperson of the Athens Olympic Organizing Committee for the 2004 Olympic Games, Gianna Daskalakis; former King Constantine of Greece, and Lambis Nikolaou, president of the Hellenic Olympic Committee and a member of the International Olympic Committee (I.O.C.) executive board.

Due to its proximity to many Olympic Games-related activities, the Cultural Center was a popular venue among Olympic visitors. It housed a large public pin-trading show, a mini festival that offered Greek foods and pastries, and an Olympic art exhibit by Rip Katsaris of St. Louis, Missouri.

The Hellenic Olympic Team, wearing hats, were escorted and assisted by volunteer parishioners, standing at back row right.

Mike C. Korologos,
I.O.C. attaché to Greek contingent.

Parishioners Demetri Tsagaris, Jim Sifantonakis, John Litsas, and Bill Rekouniotis supervised many volunteers for the mini-festival fund-raising event.

Serving as volunteers assigned to the Hellenic Olympic team were Utahns: Jim Kastanis, Mary Nackos Caputo, Sylvia Protopappas Dewey, Paraskevas Bolos, Helen Economos Draper, Ted and George Felis, Demitrios Campbell, and Elias Pylidis. Parishioner Mike C. Korologos served as the I.O.C.'s attaché to the visiting Greek contingent. Prior to the Games, Korologos was an Olympic torchbearer and, along with Nick Bapis, represented the local Greek community on a December 9, 2001, charter flight to Athens. There a delegation of Utah and national Olympic and government officials picked up the Olympic flame and delivered it to Atlanta where it began its 11,000-mile U.S. journey to Salt Lake City.

Other Events

April 22: Perry Drossos was hired as the parish's operations manager and Manoli Sargetakis was named chairperson of the community's 100th anniversary, scheduled to be observed in 2005.

The internal operation of the parish was in turmoil between June and November 2002 due to a misunderstanding regarding the ministerial and administrative duties of Deacon Elias Koucos.

August 26: At the height of the controversy, the following Parish Council resigned: Charles Beck M.D., Stephanie Chachas, Charles E. Paulos, Madelyn Bowden, Elaina Maragakis, Michael Petrogeorge, and Joseph E. Sasich. His Eminence Metropolitan Isaiah, calling the matter "a breakdown in the democratic process," dismissed the remaining council members: Dino Pappas, Paul Roumpos, Steve Gamvroulas, Basil Chelemes, Charles Cayias, Yanni Armaou, Jim Mylonakis, and Mark Vrontikis. Then, in September, he appointed an interim Parish Council consisting of David Katsanevas, president; George Adondakis, vice president; Joe Varanakis, treasurer; Billie L. Poulos, secretary; and trustees Douglas Anderson, Nick Bapis, Stan Kouris, Kay Maragakis, Ted Sargetakis, William P. Souvall, and Nick Varanakis.

Ultimately, Deacon Koucos received a letter from the Parish Council expressing its appreciation for his service to the church-community and, the following July, Metropolitan Isaiah ordained him to the priesthood in services at Prophet Elias Church.

By the end of the year, the interim council orchestrated a general assembly and parish elections, which attracted 23 candidates, a record.

September: Fr. John Kaloudis took a leave of absence from his duties, ending a 14-year stay, the longest tenure of a full-time clergyman in the history of the church. He assumed duties with the International Orthodox Christian Charities. Fr. Michael Kouremetis, formerly of Manchester, New Hampshire, who had 30 years experience as a clergyman, assumed the title of Proistamenos of Prophet Elias Church and dean of the Holy Trinity Cathedral.

2003

February: Fr. Kouremetis reported that his office at Prophet Elias Church was nearly complete and requested that Aleka DeLauro be assigned there to provide secretarial services and continue her accounting responsibilities. Fr. Kouremetis also stated he had a directive from the Metropolitan to serve

Prophet Elias Church regularly and to serve Holy Trinity Cathedral on special occasions. He suggested the Parish Council write to the Metropolitan requesting a change in his orders, a suggestion that was implemented by the board.

• Leaders of the Hellenic Heritage Campaign presented a comprehensive report to a well-attended special general assembly on March 2. This signaled the start of the restoration of Holy Trinity Cathedral and of the Hellenic Cultural Center campus. The campaign committee was expanded to include:

Nick Angelides	Kosta Katsohirakis
Douglas Anderson	David Katsanevas
Nick Bapis (chair)	George Metos
Bill Chaus	George Miller
Sam Chelemes	Vasilios Priskos
Nick Colessides	Manoli Sargetakis
Bill Drossos	Constantine J. Skedros
Perry Drossos (operations manager)	Taki Skedros
Julie Fotis	Nola Slager
Chris Gamvroulas	Margo Sotiriou
Vickie Kidman	William P. Souvall
Steve Kogianes	Jeannine Timothy
Mike C. Korologos (public relations)	Demetrios Tsagaris
Fr. Michael Kouremetis (ex-officio)	Nick Varanakis

Clergy: 1972–2005

The Rev. George Politis, 1972–
The Rev. John Kaloudis, 1987–2002
The Rev. Joachim Hatzidakis, 1987–1991
The Archimadrite Makarios Mannos, 1990–
The Rev. Constantine Palassis (retired), 1987–1993
The Rev. Dean Panagos, 1992–1995
The Rev. John Tsaras, 1996–1998
The Rev. Matthew Gilbert, 1999–
The Rev. Michael Kouremetis, 2002–
The Rev. Elias Koucos, 2003–

Parish Council Presidents: 1991–2005

Sam Chelemes, 1991–1992
Peter W. G. Cayias, 1993–1995
David Katsanevas, 1996–1997
Nick Bapis, 1998–2001
Dino Pappas, 2002
David Katsanevas (Interim), 2002
David Katsanevas, 2003
Bill Chaus, 2004–2005

2004

Aphrodite Angelides was appointed instructor of Modern Greek in the College of Humanities at the University of Utah, succeeding William D. Cocorinis who died in 2003. A native of Greece, Ms. Angelides also was a faculty member at Salt Lake City's Judge Memorial High School.

January 13: To encourage attendance at a special general assembly in February, the Hellenic Heritage Campaign Committee presented its plans to parishioners via an informative letter. The letter encapsulates the cathedral restoration project and plans for the cultural campus:

Dear Fellow Parishioners:

Our Hellenic Heritage Campaign Committee has been working diligently to move forward with the continuous progress of this project since the effort was initiated in June 1999.

<u>*Holy Trinity Cathedral Restoration.*</u> *At the special General Assembly of March 2003, the community decided to proceed with the preliminary planning and costing phase of the Holy Trinity Cathedral Restoration. This was to include architect, engineering, consultant and contractor estimates for actual construction. The plans were to be presented to a subsequent General Assembly before actual construction begins. The plans are almost completed and we are now ready to share those findings with you. The plans include proposed planning and costing details for the Cathedral Restoration including various seismic upgrades. HVAC/electrical/mechanical, and other beautification work.* **Over the coming weeks, we will be working to get final input from the community and will formulate a final recommendation. We then plan to ask for your vote and approval on February 8th to commence with the actual construction.**

<u>*Campus Planning.*</u> *At the same special General Assembly of March 2003, the community decided to proceed with the preliminary planning and costing phase of the Campus expansion. Those plans are not completed yet, be we will provide a progress report and share key findings, including:*

- *Replacement of the Sunday school rooms*
- *Development of a larger, 800-person dining facility and kitchen*
- *Creation of a full-sized gym, similar to that at Prophet Elias*
- *Museum Space*
- *Senior Living Center*
- *Parking*
- *Purchase of the Wolfe Property*

We have prepared scale models, perspective drawings, and posters of proposed Campus expansion options. These will be placed in the foyers of both church halls for your review.

To help prepare you in advance of the upcoming special General Assembly, we have arranged for the following information sessions regarding both the <u>*Cathedral Restoration*</u> *and* <u>*Campus Planning*</u>*:*

- *An information-only "Town Hall" meeting has been scheduled at Holy Trinity on Sunday, January 25 at 12:15 p.m. at the Holy Trinity gymnasium. NOTE: This will be in Greek*
- *An information-only "Town Hall" meeting has been scheduled at Prophet Elias on Wednesday, January 28 at 6:00 p.m. at the Prophet Elias hall.*
- *We are available to meet with the various church fraternal organizations.*

All this material will be presented in detail at the Special General Assembly on Sunday, February 8, 2004 at 12:30 p.m. at Holy Trinity. *These matters are of vital importance to us, to our children, and to their children. Please come and support your Hellenic Heritage Campaign project.*

Thank you for your continued support and enthusiasm. Respectfully,

—Hellenic Heritage Campaign Committee

January 19: The *Salt Lake Tribune* printed an article entitled "Boastful Chicago Charlie Makes History At Last," featuring the late Kyriakos G. Zahos, a Greek immigrant who lived in Chicago before moving to Bingham Canyon in the 1930s, where he was employed at the Bingham copper mine. A highly decorated corporal for the Greek Army during World War I, "Chicago Charlie" organized the American Flag Society and communicated regularly with some 800 young men and the 13 young women from the Bingham area who were in the U.S. Armed Forces during World War II. After the war, letters Zahos had received from the troops were encased in a war memorial monument erected at the entrance to the Bingham High School in Copperton.

In 2004, the vault housing the letters was opened and the Utah State Historical Society retrieved the 50 year-old-plus letters, many of them unopened. State historians were ecstatic with this cache of letters as it represented a rare, first-person account of the thoughts and feelings of Utahns fighting for their country. Zahos died in 1981. Later, in the spring of 2005, an article entitled "Chicago Charlie and the Bingham Canyon Victory Flag Society", written by Miriam Murphy, was published in the Spring Issue of the *Utah Historical Quarterly*.

February: Jeannine Timothy of the Hellenic Heritage Campaign Committee informed the general assembly that Holy Trinity Cathedral would be closed for restoration from June 21, 2004, until late in 2005. Divine Liturgy would be held in the Memorial Building dining hall and Sunday school classes would continue at their normal locations and times.

Letters received by Kyriakos G. Zahos, "Chicago Charlie," from servicemen during World War II were retrieved in 2004 from a monument at the original Bingham High School in Copperton, Utah.

An article in the *Salt Lake Tribune* offered insight on the restoration project:

Holy Trinity Closes Main Sanctuary For Restoration

Upgrade: During that time, services will be held in the Memorial Building next door

By Peggy Fletcher Stack

Holy Trinity Cathedral, landmark home of Salt Lake City's Greek Orthodox Church, is getting a "face-lift" or, you might say, "shoulder pads."

The main sanctuary is closing on June 21 for a $2.5 million restoration that is expected to take at least a year, said Orthodox spokesman Mike Korologos. And the exterior "just needs a new 'Sunday-go-to-meeting dress.'"

During that time, services will be held in the Memorial Building next door except during the wildly popular Greek Festival held every fall. For those two Sundays, the congregation will worship at Prophet Elias Greek Orthodox Church in Holladay.

A temporary portable altar will be erected on the east side of the hall with 350 chairs to accommodate parishioners. Valuable items, including the icon screen, will be stored in safe areas after each church service.

The structural upgrade is necessary to make the building "better suited to withstand a strong to moderate earthquake," Korologos said. The outside brick work will be improved, but it will not change the texture or look of the church, which is on the national historic register.

The parish has hired Culp Construction, which specializes in church renovations, to reinforce the bell tower, upgrade the electrical wiring, remove asbestos, add elevators, build wider landings on the main stairs and lower level entrance to the Hellenic Cultural Museum, whose office and gift shop will stay open in the Memorial Building. The sanctuary will remain relatively untouched.

The first Greek immigrants arrived in Utah around 1900 to work in the mines and railroads; within a few years the state was home to several thousand Greeks, according to a history by parishioner Constantine J. Skedros.

By 1910, Salt Lake City had a lively "Greek Town" with more than 100 Greek-owned enterprises, Skedros writes. "It was the largest Greek community between Chicago and San Francisco."

Construction on Holy Trinity Greek Orthodox Church at 279 South 300 West began with the cornerstone laying in 1925.

In addition to seismic upgrades to Holy Trinity Cathedral, the restoration includes electrical and mechanical work, beautification, and preliminary planning for expansion of the Cathedral campus.

134

The church's Byzantine architecture was modeled after the large St. Sophia Cathedral in Istanbul, Turkey, the so-called "Mother Church" for the Greek Orthodox. It cost $150,000.

In 1950, the Hellenic Memorial Cultural Center was added next to the cathedral to serve the church's educational, recreational and social needs.

It was "dedicated to the memory of the young men from the [Utah] Greek community who made the supreme sacrifice for their country in World War I and II," Skedros writes.

Twenty-seven years later, the church added the Memorial Building with additional dining facilities, a new kitchen area, and space for parish offices. This is the site of the popular Greek Festival, which was launched in 1976 and has become one of the most successful ethnic events in the city.

Holy Trinity has hosted several world-class events including a special meeting of the Dalai Lama, spiritual and political leader of exiled Tibetans, during his 2001 visit to Utah.

In April 1986, Archbishop Iakovos, primate of the Greek Orthodox Archdiocese of North and South America, came to Utah. Iakovos elevated Holy Trinity's status from church to "cathedral," Skedros writes, which was "a most significant honor for the Greek Orthodox parishioners of the Salt Lake Valley and Utah."

—*Salt Lake Tribune*
June 6, 2004

This 1924 key to front gate of Holy Trinity Cathedral was found by Culp Construction workers in July 2004.

June 4-5: Mary Royal, representing Holy Trinity Cathedral, won the $2,000 first place prize at the National St. John Chrysostom Oratorical Festival in Detroit, Michigan. Dallas Holbeck, Prophet Elias Church, won $500 for his work in the junior division.

In July, ground-breaking ceremonies were held for Holy Trinity Cathedral's restoration.

September 17: Ted J. Speros, restaurateur, civic leader and former Parish Council president, received the T. K. McCarthey Silver Hope Award for "a lifetime of community service" from the Multiple Sclerosis Society of Utah.

November: General chairman Manoli Sargetakis gave a report to the general assembly on the parish's 100th anniversary celebration, planned for October 28–30, 2005.

Announced as chairs of the primary committees were: Georgia Katsanevas, hospitality night; Steve Kogianes, grand gala; John Johnson, government relations; Jenny Skedros, luncheon; Fr. Kouremetis, religious affairs; Mike C. Korologos, centennial commemorative book; John Saltas, 2005 commemorative album; and Michael Bapis and Ted Sargetakis, sponsorships.

As the Greek community planned for its 100th anniversary to be celebrated in 2005, it had become recognized as the "Orthodoxy focal point" envisioned by Fr. Steven Katsaris in 1956.

This proposed architectural concept of a Holy Trinity Greek
Orthodox Campus on church property looking southeast from the
corner of 200 South and 300 West excites the imagination. Using
the cathedral as the anchor, the rendering uses a Greek village
plaza-like setting to complement facilities housing Sunday school
classrooms, multi-purpose center/gymnasium, museum, dining
space, church offices, large kitchen/storage area, underground
parking, apartment units and retail outlets at street level. This is a
conceptual design only. The concept was presented to the
community's Hellenic Heritage Campaign Committee in July 2005.
Any development of the church property will be subject to
community input, need, priorities and funding before any plans are
finalized.

Rendering provided by GSBS Architects and CJK Design.

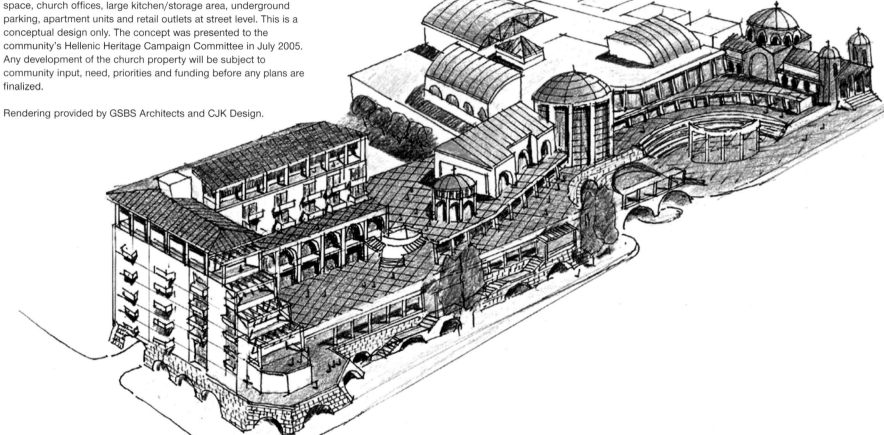

Chapter 10

Year-Long Centennial Celebration, 2005

The pride of 100 years of overcoming hardships and controversy, envisioning a Greek Orthodox community with faith, and celebrating heroic accomplishments has been realized in 2005. This year culminates in celebrations harkening back to our heritage of hard work and resourcefulness.

Metropolitan Isaiah of the Denver Diocese.

Fr. Michael Kouremetis set the tone for the community's high profile, multi-faceted, year-long centennial observance when he presented the invocation for the inauguration of Jon M. Huntsman, Jr., as governor of Utah on January 3. In that regard, Fr. Kouremetis wrote parishioners: "After 100 years as a community in this valley, we were honored with a personal invitation from Governor Huntsman to give the invocation at his inauguration. We thank Governor Huntsman for his inclusiveness and wish him strength and good health in undertaking his new position as the leader of our fine State of Utah. Our Greek Orthodox community has received great publicity from participation in this event both locally and on a national level."

2005

January 14–17: A variety of social and religious events and dozens of games during the Metropolis of Denver GOYA Basketball Tournament held in Salt Lake City attracted 637 young athletes. His Eminence Metropolitan Isaiah of Denver was an honored guest. Boys and girls teams hailed from Utah, New Mexico, Colorado, Texas, Oklahoma, Missouri, and Arkansas. The event was chaired by Michael Daskalas and

The Holy Trinity - Prophet Elias basketball team played in the Metropolis of Denver GOYA tournament held in Salt Lake city in January 2005.

served as a fund-raising event for a Serbian youth camp in Kosovo. Most games were played at the Open Court facility in Lehi, Utah, with the championship round played at Salt Lake City's Delta Center, home of the Utah Jazz of the National Basketball Association (N.B.A.). A special Sunday liturgy was held at the Grand America Hotel and the awards banquet that night attracted 795 participants.

February 13: A special general assembly was informed that in the Consolidated Appropriations Act for fiscal year 2005 passed by the U.S. Congress, $75,000 was awarded to the Hellenic Cultural Association "for exhibit and program development at the Hellenic Cultural Museum." The money represented the first phase of an effort to seek as much as $3.5

million in federal funding for the museum. Spearheading this fund-raising effort were Andrew Manatos, Washington D.C., and Salt Lake parishioners Paul Roumpos, George Hatsis, D.D.S., Jim Kastanis, and Bill Drossos. The community pledged its support. Funds for a cultural museum are designated as a part of the community's Hellenic Heritage Campaign.

March: Twelve members of the parish's Sunday schools won awards in the 2005 St. John Chrysostom Oratorical competition: Junior Division, first place—Pilar Pappas and Emanuel Liodakis; second place—Andrew Kithas and Ana Pantelides; third place—Katina Papadakis and Leia Sergakis. Senior Division, first place—Catherine Dimas and Danielle Hillas; second place—Hrysoula Papadakis and Gus Paras; third place—Dorothann Dinas and Larissa Beck.

March: Parishioner Bill Mouskondis, chairman of Nicholas & Co., a Salt Lake City-based food service distribution company, was awarded the Utah Restaurant Association Lifetime Achievement Award.

March: The community's Enosis Dance Group received the Founders Special Achievement Award in the advanced senior division of the Greek Folk Dance Festival in Ontario, California. Under the direction of Fr. Kouremetis, this troupe consisted of: Matthew Caputo, Anastacia Georgelas, Paul Liacopoulos, Crystal Litsas, Vasilis Lyhnakis, Nicolette O'Leary, Andrea Pappas, Kate Pappas, Michael Parenti, Georgiann Pino, John Pylidis, Alaina Stockslager, Faye

Tsagaris, Chris Tsoutsounakis, Artemis Vamianakis, Nicholas Vamianakis, Alexis Varanakis, and musicians Kosta Fillipakis and Greg Manouselis.

March, April, and May: Parish families/households posed for photographs that would be published in a first-ever pictorial directory of the church family.

April 9: The parish was prominently represented by dozens of members on Team Hermes that participated in a community service project called "Walk Around the World." The fund-raising walk supported multiple sclerosis research.

April 24: On the actual 100th anniversary date of the Greek church-community in Salt Lake City, Metropolitan Isaiah and Fr. Michael Kouremetis opened the container discovered in January during the extensive restoration work on the cathedral. The restoration included removal of the altar, which exposed a large slab of concrete. When workers removed the concrete they found a circular opening that housed a small copper container. Inside the container they found a selection of very small pieces of religious relics. They also discovered the year 1905 etched on the underside of the container lid.

These discoveries validated the answer to a question that had arisen in the midst of the planning for the church community's 100th anniversary observances and the compilation of information related to its early history. That question was whether Holy Trinity Cathedral had been consecrated (declared holy for religious use).

 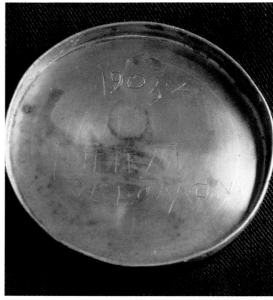

A copper tin, containing very small pieces of religious relics, was found under Holy Trinity altar during reconstruction.

The date 1905 is etched on the underside of the container's lid.

"She told me that she remembered, as a young girl of 13 in 1925, that members of the congregation from the original Holy Trinity Church carried icons and many other religious items from the old church to the new Holy Trinity Church, which was located on 300 South 200 West, a distance of about two blocks."

—Barbara Floor Kalantzes
Recalling story told by her mother-in-law, Olga Cozakos Kalantzes.
Greek Oral History Collection

Ecumenical Patriarch Bartholomew of Constantinople (Istanbul).

Archbishop Demetrios of the Greek Orthodox Archdiocese of the United States.

Metropolitan Isaiah concluded that the relics in the container were part of the consecration of the church. His conclusion was reinforced by the date on the lid, which coincided with the known construction date of the original Greek church in the city. In August 1925, the container and its prized relics, which had been removed from the original church site, were placed under the altar of the then-new Holy Trinity Church when it was consecrated. Prior to the conclusion of the Cathedral restoration project, the container and its contents were returned to the place where they were found, under the altar.

May 7: Art, music, food, and fellowship were the order of the day at the 100th Anniversary Music and Art Fest at Prophet Elias Church. The event featured an exhibition of artwork by Russian artist Yevgeniy Zolotsev, parish artist Syd Colessides, and the modern style icon artwork of the parish's Victor Maritsas. Musical groups, soloists, and a concert of Greek sacred and folk music by the Prophet Elias Choir, directed by Paul Maritsas supplemented the artistic fare.

May 13: More than 150 visitors joined Utah parishioners at meetings, social activities, and a banquet that highlighted the Denver Metropolis Clergy Laity Assembly and Philoptochos Conference in Salt Lake City. The conference was under the direction of Fr. Kouremetis, Bill Chaus, Nick Varanakis, and Mark Vrontikis. Philoptochos Society planners were Shelly Anderson,

Elizabeth Beck, Stephanie Chachas, Angela Petrogeorge, Georgiann Pino, Nola Slager, Margo Sotiriou, Ann Varanakis, and Sophie Wondolowski.

June 19: In a special observance of the church's name day, the parish families enjoyed a celebration, "A Taste of Greece," in the Hellenic Memorial Cultural Center. The event centered on the observance of the Pentecost Holy Trinity name day, which had not been celebrated in such a manner for several years. Chairpersons for the event were Jenny Skedros and Sophie Wondolowski.

June 9–27: The Prophet Elias Church Choir, under the direction of Paul Maritsas, made a pilgrimage to Greece where it participated in six concerts and three liturgies at some of the country's most historically prominent venues. The trip included evening concerts in Iraklion, Crete; and at the acoustically acclaimed amphitheater at Naufplion, in Pyrgos, Patras, Corinth/Megara, and Athens.

July 24: The annual church picnic and barbecue had a 100th anniversary emphasis and attracted many families and youngsters to the shady grounds adjacent to Prophet Elias Church.

September 9–10–11: The annual Greek Festival and related 5-K health walk, 5-K and 10-K races (called The Greek Classic) enjoyed heightened interest and participation due to the added public exposure the community was generating by virtue of its 100th anniversary activities.

140

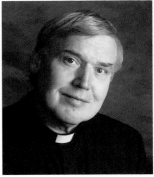

Deacon Anatoli Kireiev.

Clergymen serving the Greek Orthodox Church of Greater Salt Lake in 2005 are Rev. Elias Koucos, left, Rev. George Politis, Rev. Michael Kouremetis, Rev. Mathew Gilbert, and Deacon Anatoli Kireiev in photo to the right.

October 28–30: The Greek Orthodox community of Salt Lake City observed its 100th anniversary in a series of well-orchestrated activities —ranging from historic photo displays to grand banquets—that paid tribute to the early Greek immigrants as well as to the succeeding generations.

The legacy of Greek immigrant faith and fervor continues to this day and will be expressed by future generations in the Intermountain West and beyond. This is but the first 100 years of a shining Greek Orthodox presence in the heart of the Wasatch Mountains and the Greater Salt Lake Valley.

Copperfield, 1924. Among the many mining communities, such as Highland Boy, Copperton, and others in Bingham Canyon, was the Greek enclave of Copperfield. The row houses and public buildings of the main street are all gone now—only memories of the community where Christ Pappasotiriou brought his bride, Helen Zes, from Greece to begin their life together.

The Pappasotiriou Family:
Living the American Dream...with a Song

Dad loved to sing "God Bless America" because he was so happy to be in this country.

—*Margo Sotiriou*

Christ Pappasotiriou and Helen Zes on their wedding day in 1929.

Christ Pappasotiriou was born in Levithi, Greece in 1885 and died in 1963. He worked in the fields and finished high school. At the age of 22, he migrated to America and traveled directly to the gloves-off mining town of Copperfield in Bingham Canyon, Utah, to join his brother, Stavro, and other immigrants.

He worked in the copper mine for one day—long enough to convince him that mine work was not for him. He joined his brother in operating the Independent Grocery, Inc., which catered to miners and their families. When Stavro returned to Greece to care for family members there, Christ took over the market in conjunction with partner George Pappasideris.

"Dad always sent money to his family in Greece because his sisters needed dowries," says Christ's daughter Margo, a retired schoolteacher. He also managed to earn enough money to become owner of the 13-unit Copperfield Apartment building. It included the Dianna Movie Theater that later became a bar-restaurant. He also purchased some nearby auto garages. The property was located a few yards from the copper mining operation's yawning open pit.

In 1929, Christ visited his homeland to see a sister who was suffering from tuberculosis. Upon his arrival, he discovered his mother had arranged a marriage for him to one Helen Zes, born in 1903, a girl 18 years his junior. She

Editor's note: Publication of "Faith and Fervor" was made possible by a generous contribution from the family of the late Christ and Helen Pappasotiriou (Sotiriou). The story of this family personifies the essence of this book: The saga of thousands of Greeks immigrants who arrived in Utah during the early part of the Twentieth Century with not much more than a hope for a better life for their families.

143

agreed to the arranged marriage, as she—like Christ had done in 1906—was anxious to leave the rigors of the farm fields for the storied opportunities in America.

The couple traveled on the steamer *Saturnia*, arriving in New York on January 1, 1931, and in Copperfield a few weeks later. Returning to the fledgling business enterprise Christ had established, the couple worked at the grocery store and began to raise a family that came to include Gus, born in 1931, Tommie, Margo, and Leo.

"I was born in a hotel room, above a beer joint and across the street from a house of ill repute," laughs Christ's second son, Tommie.

A 1984 family portrait shows, Cynthia, front left, Alexander, Helen, Gus, and Tommie; Leo, back left, Margo, Elena, Antoinette, and Chris.

Tommie's memories of his early years in Bingham Canyon are vivid. "Gus and I would ride in the back of dad's Chevrolet pickup truck and help him deliver groceries in Dinkyville, in the upper reaches of Copperfield," he recalls. "And I remember watching Western films in our small theater. More than once, older brother Gus and I would walk from Copperfield, through the two- and one-half mile Bingham tunnel, to lower Bingham to play basketball at the Gemmel Club, a gymnasium."

One of Margo's memories deals with playing jump-rope while in the first grade at Copperfield School. "We would call out a month with every jump and you were supposed to stop on the month of your birthday. You know, I didn't know my birthday month. To us, observing our Greek Name Days was more important than our birthdays."

Margo also recalls, "Every day at 3 o'clock our mother would insist we take a nap. That was because between 3 and 3:30 in the afternoon they'd blast the dynamite at the mine pit. When they did that, our apartment would shake, windows would rattle, and things would fall off the table. Mom didn't want us outside. That was another reason she insisted we move from Copperfield to Salt Lake City."

By the time the family moved from Copperfield in 1945, members were familiar with Salt Lake City, since they had visited often to attend Sunday church services. "It was a 28-mile drive that took an hour and a half-drive, each way, not because of traffic but because the truck couldn't go any faster," says Margo. "I would ride with mom in the front of dad's 1930 Chevy pickup and the boys would be in the back. It was a day-long trip so mom would prepare a picnic lunch of *keftethes* (meatballs) that we would eat at Pioneer Park, across from the church, after the services."

With the proceeds from the sale of his properties in Copperfield to the mining company, Christ opened a grocery store in 1946 at 242 East 300 South. He called it the Sunny Market. Later it became known as the Broadway Shopping Center and boasted of being the first combined grocery store and pharmacy in Utah.

All of Christ's and Helen's children—Gus, Tommie, Margo, and Leo—worked at the store, alongside their dad. "Mom stayed home," says Margo because "she did not see a need to learn much English. Most of the people she associated with were Greeks. But, I'll tell you, she was really proud of the fact that she became an American citizen; so was Dad." Helen died in 1990.

In 1972, the family market was razed and the multi-million dollar Broadway Shopping Center was built on the site. It offered office and retail space as well as the grocery/pharmacy operations.

The close-knit nature of the family was reflected by the fact that the children followed their father's wishes—all have been active in the Greek Orthodox Church and all four graduated from college. Gus, Tommie, and Leo became pharmacists and Leo continued his studies and became a dermatologist. Margo became a teacher and taught for 35 years in elementary grades in the Salt Lake City School system. The foursome shortened their name to Sotiriou when Gus and Tommie entered the military during the Korean War. "We couldn't find any record of a priest—'Pappa'—among relatives in our generation, so we made spelling the name easy on everybody," says Tommie.

As irony would have it, the current Broadway Shopping Center grocery/pharmacy has a Chris Sotiriou behind the counter. He is the son of Gus, who died in 2001, and Antoinette. And, in keeping with Greek family tradition, he is named after his grandfather. Gus' other child, Elena, was killed in an automobile accident at age 18 in 1987—"the saddest day of our lives . . . she was so young," acknowledges Leo.

In another throwback to the family ways of old, Chris is joined in the pharmacy by his wife, Parinaz, while the children of Leo and Cynthia—Alexander, Michael, Elysia, and Stephen—periodically earn spending money working the grocery side, when they find time between school studies and church activities.

No doubt, Christ and Helen Pappasotiriou would be proud of their legacy . . . and they would be singing "God Bless America."

Tommie Sotiriou at age 6 on Copperfield's main street.

Appendix

Salt Lake parishioners ordained as deacons or into the priesthood in the Greek Orthodox Church since 1944

The Rev. Nicholas J. Velis, 1944

The Rev. Angelo Gavalas, 1950

The Rev. Nick Manousakis, 1971

The Rev. George Politis
   Deacon and Priest, 1972

Archimandrite Makarios Mannos
   Deacon, 1975
   Priest, 1984
   Archimandrite, 1998

The Rev. Luke G. Kontgas, 1985

Deacon Peter Alex, 1986

The Rev. Joseph Strezelki
   Deacon and Priest, 1988

Deacon Anatoli Kireiev, 1990

The Rev. Gus Petrogeorge
   Deacon, 1989
   Priest, 1990

The Rev. Mario Giannopoulos
   Deacon and Priest, 1992

The Rev. Tony Savas
   Deacon, 1996
   Priest, 1997

Deacon Constantine Lazarakis, 2002

The Rev. Elias Koucos
   Deacon, 1994
   Priest, 2003

Greek Church Chanters, 1905–2005

Salt Lake Greek Church records show the following served as chanters at Holy Trinity and Prophet Elias Greek Orthodox churches between 1905 and 2005:

1905	*Theodore Moutis*	*Holy Trinity*
	Mr. Politis	*Holy Trinity*
1914–1952	*James Demetriadis (Demas)*	*Holy Trinity*
1930–1935	*John Ahladas*	*Holy Trinity*
1936–1939	*Constantine Milenopoulos*	*Holy Trinity*
1945–1960	*Louis Flangas*	*Holy Trinity*
1950–1970	*Sakis Sakellariou*	*Holy Trinity*
1960–1965	*Peter Gamvroulas*	*Holy Trinity*
1969–1970	*John Nikas*	*Prophet Elias*
1969–present	*Gregory Karahalios*	*Prophet Elias*
1969–1975	*George Politis*	*Prophet Elias*
1970–1978	*George Gerontis*	*Holy Trinity/ Prophet Elias*
1970–1985	*Andrew Venezelos*	*Holy Trinity*
1978–present	*Peter Gamvroulas*	*Holy Trinity*
1978–present	*Chris Gamvroulas*	*Holy Trinity*
1990	*Keven Hill*	*Prophet Elias*
1990–2000	*George Pulos*	*Prophet Elias*
1990–present	*Dean Athens*	*Prophet Elias*
1990–present	*Bobbie Marcooles*	*Holy Trinity*

Serving as volunteer chanters at Holy Trinity from the 1920s to the 1950s were:

Chris Dokos	*Steve Stavropoulos*
George Hatsis	*Gus Theonas*
Harry Liapis	*James Tsakalos*
James C. Skedros	*Nick Tsimpoukis*

Books and Directories

Cononelos, Louis J. *In Search of Gold Paved Streets: Greek Immigrant Labor in the Far West, 1900–1920.* Masters Thesis, University of Utah, 1979, AMS Press, NY, 1989.

Papanikolas, Helen Zeese. "Immigrant Minorities in the Great War," *Utah State Historical Quarterly*, 1990; "Toil and Rage in a New Land, the Greek Immigrant in Utah." *Utah Historical Quarterly.* 1970, Spring.

Saloutos, Theodore. "Greeks in the Great Plains and Rocky Mountain West." *Pacific Historical Review.* February, 1980.

Salt Lake City Directory. 1900–1903.

Skedros, Constantine J. *Computer History of Greek WWI Veterans.* 1990. Holy Trinity Cathedral, Salt Lake City, Utah.

Files

Hellenic Cultural Association (H.C.A.) Library Files of newspaper articles referring to Greek individuals and events. 1907–1950.

Deseret News	*Ogden Standard Examiner*
Herald Republican	*Salt Lake Herald*
Intermountain Republican	*Salt Lake Telegram*
Kalifornia Greek Newspaper	*Salt Lake Tribune*

Skedros, Constantine J. My personal files from 1948 to the present include: a collection of letters, programs, reports about church activities and meetings, newspaper articles, obituaries, etc. These documents and materials were resources used in this history.

Minutes

Boards of Trustees and general assemblies. 1905–1950. Minutes written in Greek. In 1954, James C. Dokos (deceased) made a brief translation into English. The commemorative book for the Greek Orthodox Church community's 50th Anniversary, 1955, was based upon those translations, which have since been lost.

Parish Council and general assembly minutes in English since 1956. Some minutes are missing. Some letters and related documents are missing from existing minutes. I have read all the minutes dating from 1956 to the present.

Oral Histories

The Greek Oral History Collection, Manuscripts Division, J. Willard Marriott Library, University of Utah, Salt Lake City, Utah. Personal tape-recorded quotes from Greek immigrants and second-generation Greek Americans.

Records

Holy Trinity Greek Orthodox Church records of all sacraments from 1905 to the present are available. In the early years, record keeping by the clergy was not consistent. Gaps exist in a number of those years.

Holy Trinity Greek Orthodox Church-sponsored groups— athletic, dance, choirs, fraternal organizations— minutes, records, interviews of members.

Salt Lake City newspapers
Third District Judicial Court
Utah State Archives

Name Index

R